THE BEST TEST PREPARATION FOR THE
ADVANCED PLACEMENT EXAMINATIONS

For Both
MICROECONOMICS &
MACROECONOMICS

Richard Sattora, M.S.

Economics Instructor
Pittsford Mendon High School, Pittsford, NY

**Recipient of the "Blue Ribbon Teacher of
Economics" award from the
Federal Reserve Bank of Dallas**

D1305102

Research & Education Association
61 Ethel Road West • Piscataway, New Jersey 08854
Dr. M. Fogiel, Director

The Best Test Preparation for the
ADVANCED PLACEMENT (AP) EXAMINATIONS
for both MICROECONOMICS AND MACROECONOMICS

Printed in the United States of America

Library of Congress Control Number 2003107252

International Standard Book Number 0-87891-459-5

REA is a registered trademark of Research & Education Association

Research & Education Association
61 Ethel Road West
Piscataway, New Jersey 08854

REA supports the effort to conserve and
protect environmental resources by
printing on recycled papers.

CONTENTS

About Research & Education Association

Research & Education Association (REA) is an organization of educators, scientists, and engineers specializing in various academic fields. Founded in 1959 with the purpose of disseminating the most recently developed scientific information to groups in industry, government, and universities, REA has since become a successful and highly respected publisher of study aids, test preps, handbooks, and reference works.

REA's Test Preparation series includes study guides for all academic levels in almost all disciplines. Research & Education Association publishes test preps for students who have not yet completed high school, as well as high school students preparing to enter college. Students from countries around the world seeking to attend college in the United States will find the assistance they need in REA's publications. For college students seeking advanced degrees, REA publishes test preps for many major graduate school admission examinations in a wide variety of disciplines, including engineering, law, and medicine. Students at every level, in every field, with every ambition can find what they are looking for among REA's publications.

While most test preparation books present only a few practice tests that bear little resemblance to the actual exams, REA's series presents tests that accurately depict the official exams in both degree of difficulty and types of questions. REA's practice tests are always based upon the most recently administered exams, and include every type of question that can be expected on the actual exams.

REA's publications and educational materials are highly regarded and continually receive an unprecedented amount of praise from professionals, instructors, librarians, parents, and students. Our authors are as diverse as the subject matter represented in the books we publish. They are well-known in their respective fields and serve on the faculties of prestigious high schools, colleges, and universities throughout the United States and Canada.

Acknowledgments

In addition to our author, we would like to thank Dr. Max Fogiel, President, for his overall guidance, which brought this publication to completion; Larry B. Kling, Quality Control Manager, for supervising development; Gianfranco Origliato, Editorial Assistant, for coordinating development; John Slonim, M.Ed., for verifying the manuscript's technical accuracy; Graves Editorial Service for copyediting; Michael C. Cote for typesetting the manuscript; and Jeff LoBalbo, Senior Graphic Designer, for post-production electronic prepping. We also wish to acknowledge the editorial contributions of Catherine Battos and Mark Zipkin.

INDEPENDENT STUDY SCHEDULES

STUDY SCHEDULE FOR THE AP EXAM IN MICROECONOMICS

The following study schedule will help you become thoroughly prepared for the AP Microeconomics exam. Although the schedule is designed as a six-week study program, it can be condensed into three weeks if less time is available by combining two weeks into one. Be sure to set aside enough time each day for studying purposes. If you choose the six-week program, you should plan to study for at least one hour per day. If you choose the three-week program, you should plan to study for at least two hours per day. Keep in mind that the more time you devote to studying for the Microeconomics exam, the more prepared and confident you will be on the day of the exam.

Week	Activity
1	Read and study the introduction on the following pages. Then, take and score the Microeconomics practice test to determine your strengths and weaknesses. You should have someone familiar with economics score your responses to Section II of the exam. When you grade your exam, you should determine which types of questions cause you the most difficulty, as this will help you determine the areas requiring the most study. For example, if you incorrectly answer a number of questions dealing with Costs and Cost Analysis, you should carefully study the related sections in the review. Begin studying for the exam by reading the Basic Economic Concepts Review and AP Microeconomics Course Structure.
2	Continue your review by reading and studying the Key Terms section associated with Microeconomics, the Interaction of Supply and Demand, and stop after completing the section on the Long-Run Costs of Production.
3	Read and study the remainder of the Microeconomics review, beginning with the Four Production Market Models and ending with Merger Types.
4	Study the appendices and the glossary of economics terms.
5	Take and score the Microeconomics practice test once more. Refer back to your original score and Section II answers (and responses from the individual who graded it) only after you complete the test.
6	Read through the entire Microeconomics review, focusing primarily on the material with which you are weakest. You may also want to consult your textbook for additional support.

STUDY SCHEDULE FOR THE AP EXAM IN MACROECONOMICS

The following study schedule will help you become thoroughly prepared for the AP Macroeconomics exam. Although the schedule is designed as a six-week study program, it can be condensed into three weeks if less time is available by collapsing two weeks into one. Be sure to set aside enough time each day for studying purposes. If you choose the six-week program, you should plan to study for at least one hour per day. If you choose the three-week program, you should plan to study for at least two hours per day. Keep in mind that the more time you devote to studying for the Macroeconomics exam, the more prepared and confident you will be on the day of the exam.

Week	Activity
1	Read and study the introduction on the following pages. Then, take and score the Macroeconomics practice test to determine your strengths and weaknesses. You should have someone familiar with economics score your responses to Section II of the exam. When you grade your exam, you should determine what types of questions cause you the most difficulty, as this will help you determine the areas requiring the most study. For example, if you incorrectly answer a number of questions dealing with Monetary Policy, you should carefully study the relevant sections in the review.
	Begin studying for the exam by reading the Basic Economic Concepts Review and AP Macroeconomics Construct.
2	Continue your review by reading and studying the Key Terms section associated with Macroeconomics, Measuring Economic Performance, and stop after completing the section on IDM, Interest Rates, and AD/AS Model.
3	Read and study the remainder of the Macroeconomics review, beginning with the Aggregate Demand/Aggregate Supply Model and ending with Currency Exchange Rates.
4	Study the appendices and the glossary of economics terms.
5	Take and score the Macroeconomics practice test once more. Refer back to your original score and Section II answers (and responses from the individual who graded it) only after you complete the test.
6	Read through the entire Macroeconomics review, focusing primarily on the material with which you are weakest. You may also want to consult your textbook for additional support.

STUDY SCHEDULE FOR AP EXAMS IN BOTH MICROECONOMICS AND MACROECONOMICS

The following study schedule will help you become thoroughly prepared for taking both AP Economics exams in succession. Although the schedule is designed as a six-week study program, it can be condensed into three weeks if less time is available by combining two weeks into one. Be sure to set aside enough time each day for studying purposes. If you choose the six-week program, you should plan to study for at least one hour per day. If you choose the three-week program, you should plan to study for at least two hours per day. Keep in mind that the more time you devote to studying for the AP Economics exams, the more prepared and confident you will be on the day of the exams.

Week	Activity
1	Read and study the introduction on the following pages. Then, take and score the practice tests in this book to determine your strengths and weaknesses. You should have someone familiar with economics score your responses to Section II of the exams. When you grade your exams, you should determine which types of questions cause you the most difficulty, as this will help you determine which areas to review most thoroughly. For example, if you incorrectly answer a number of questions dealing with Costs and Cost Analysis, you should carefully study the relevant sections in the review. Begin studying for both exams by reading the Basic Economics Concepts Review.
2	Continue your review by reading and studying the Microeconomics review, paying particular attention to the Key Terms.
3	Read and study the Macroeconomics review, again paying close attention to the Key Terms.
4	Study the Appendices and the glossary of Economics terms.
5	Take and score the practice tests once more. Refer back to your original score and Section II answers (and responses from the individual who graded it) only after you complete the tests.
6	Read through the entire Micro- and Macroeconomics reviews, focusing primarily on the material with which you are weakest. You may also want to consult your textbook for additional support.

▼

PASSING THE
AP ECONOMICS
EXAMS

PASSING THE AP ECONOMICS EXAMS

ABOUT THIS BOOK

The purpose of this book is to provide a review for the Advanced Placement Economics Examinations written in high school vernacular. Our mission is to translate economics to a level understandable to the average student.

One full-length practice exam is included for both the Macroeconomics exam and the Microeconomics exam. Use them, along with the detailed explanations of answers, to help determine your strengths and weaknesses, and to prepare yourself to score well on the actual exams.

ABOUT THE ADVANCED PLACEMENT PROGRAM

The Advanced Placement program is designed to provide high school students with the opportunity to pursue college-level studies. The AP Economics course has two components (Macroeconomics and Microeconomics), each of which is tested and graded separately.

Students are expected to gain college-level skills and acquire college-level knowledge of economics through the AP course. Upon completion of the course, students may take the AP exam for Macroeconomics, Microeconomics, or both. Test results are used to grant course credit and/or determine placement level in the subject when entering college.

AP exams are offered every May. The exam schedule allows everyone the opportunity to take both exams on the same day—Macroeconomics in the morning, Microeconomics in the afternoon. For more information contact Educational Testing Service or the College Board:

AP Services – Educational Testing Service
P.O. Box 6671
Princeton, NJ 08541-6671
Phone: (609) 771-7300
Fax: (609) 530-0482
E-mail: apexams@ets.org
Web site: http://www.collegeboard.com

ABOUT THE AP ECONOMICS EXAMS

The two components of the AP Economics course are tested and graded separately. It is possible to receive a qualified rating (3 or greater) on one exam and not the other. Also, one fee of $77.00 entitles the examinee to take one or both of the exams. Each exam carries three college credit hours, although many schools require a grade of 4 or 5 to replace their introductory macro or micro course. The two separate exams consist of the following:

The exams are 2 hours and 10 minutes long. Each section in each exam is completed separately. You will have 70 minutes to answer 60 multiple choice questions, worth 67% of your final grade. Each correct answer is worth one point, and each incorrect answer takes away 1/4 point.

The free-response section is 60 minutes long and has three questions. You will have a ten-minute reading section, followed by 50 minutes to answer the questions. The first is long and worth 15 points, and the second and third (short) essay questions are worth 15 total. The points for this section comprise 33% of the exam.

AP MICROECONOMICS EXAM DISTRIBUTION

I.   Basic economic concepts (8–12%)
   1.   Scarcity: the nature of economic systems
   2.   Opportunity costs and production possibilities
   3.   Specialization and comparative advantage
   4.   The functions of any economic system (what, how, and for whom to produce)

II.   The nature and functions of product markets (60–70%)
   1.   Supply and demand (15–20%)
      a.   Price and quantity determination
      b.   Basic manipulation of supply and demand, including ceilings and floors
   2.   Models of consumer choice (5–10%)
      a.   Consumer choice behind the demand curve
      b.   Elasticity
   3.   Firm production, costs, and revenues (10–15%)
      a.   Marginal product and diminishing returns
      b.   Average and marginal costs and revenues
      c.   Long-run costs and economies of scale

    4.   Product pricing and outputs, both in the individual firm and in the market (25–30%)
        a.   Perfect competition
        b.   Imperfect competition
           •   Monopoly
           •   Oligopoly
           •   Monopolistic competition
    5.   Efficiency and government policy toward imperfect competition (5–10%)

III.   Factor markets (10–15%)
    1.   Derived factor demand
    2.   Determination of wages and other factor prices

IV.   Efficiency, equity, and the role of government (8–12%)
    1.   Market failures
        a.   Externalities
        b.   Public goods
    2.   Distribution of income

AP MACROECONOMICS EXAM DISTRIBUTION

I.   Basic economic concepts (5–10%)
    1.   Scarcity: the nature of economic systems
    2.   Opportunity costs and production possibilities
    3.   Specialization and comparative advantage
    4.   The functions of any economic system (what, how, and for whom to produce)
    5.   Demand, supply, price determination
II.   Measurement of economic performance (8–12%)
    1.   Gross national product, gross domestic product, and national income concepts
    2.   Inflation and price indices
    3.   Unemployment
III. National income and price determination (70–75%)
    1.   Aggregate supply (8–12%)
        a.   Classical analysis
        b.   Keynesian analysis
        c.   Rational expectations
    2.   Aggregate demand (25–35%)
        a.   Circular flow
        b.   Components of aggregate demand

    c.   Multiplier
    d.   Fiscal policy
    e.   Monetary policy

3.   Money and banking (10–15%)
    a.   Definition of money and its creation
    b.   Tools of central bank policy

4.   Fiscal-monetary mix (10–15%)
    a.   Interaction of fiscal and monetary policies
    b.   Monetarist-Keynesian controversy
    c.   Deficits

5.   Trade-offs between inflation and unemployment (8–10%)
    a.   Long run versus short run
    b.   Supply shocks
    c.   Role of expectations

IV. Economic growth (4–6%)

V.   International finance, exchange rates, and balance of payments (4–6%)
1.   International policy
2.   International finance, exchange rates, and balance of payments

ABOUT OUR TOPICAL REVIEW

As mentioned earlier, this review is designed to prepare you for success on the College Board's AP Economics Exams. Therefore, an entire year's work has been distilled into the leanest preparation manual possible to ensure victory on exam day. This text is aimed at students serious about improving their likelihood of success through hard work and attention to the key elements to be tested. This text will also help a student prepare for daily classroom success as well. Students have a variety of learning styles that are not always met by classroom teachers, so this text will serve well as a supplement to daily classroom learning. Components of this review have been field-tested in the classroom by students of varying capacity, and all can attest to their improved performance both in the classroom, as well as on the exam; they average nearly one full point higher than the nation!

SCORING REA's PRACTICE EXAMS

Scoring the Multiple-Choice Sections

For each multiple-choice section, use this formula to calculate your raw score:

_____	− (_____	× 1/4) =	_____
Number Correct	Number Wrong		Multiple-Choice
(out of 60)			Score (weighted)

Scoring the Free-Response Sections

For the Macroeconomics exam's free-response section, use this formula to calculate your raw score:

Question 1 _____ × $1^{1}/_{2}$ = _____
    (out of 10)   (weighted)

Question 2 _____ × $1^{1}/_{2}$ = _____
    (out of 5)   (weighted)

Question 3 _____ × $1^{7}/_{8}$ = _____
    (out of 4)   (weighted)

_____	+	_____	+	_____	=	_____
Question 1		Question 2		Question 3		Macroeconomics
(weighted)		(weighted)		(weighted)		Free-Response
						Score (weighted)

For the Microeconomics exam's free-response section, use this formula to calculate your raw score:

Question 1 _____ × $1^{7}/_{8}$ = _____
    (out of 8)   (weighted)

Question 2 _____ × $1^{1}/_{4}$ = _____
    (out of 6)   (weighted)

Question 3 _____ × $1^{1}/_{4}$ = _____
    (out of 6)   (weighted)

_____	+	_____	+	_____	=	_____
Question 1		Question 2		Question 3		Microeconomics
(weighted)		(weighted)		(weighted)		Free-Response
						Score (weighted)

The Composite Score

To obtain your composite score for each exam, use the following method:

_____ + _____ = _____
  Multiple-Choice   Free-Response   Composite Score
  Weighted Score   Weighted Score

Use the following chart to approximate your AP score for each exam:

AP Grade Conversion Chart

Final Score Range*	AP Grade
70 – 90	5
54 – 69	4
42 – 53	3
28 – 41	2
0 – 27	1

SCORING THE OFFICIAL EXAMS

Weighted Multiple-Choice + Weighted Free-Response = Total Composite Score (90)

The College Board creates a formula (which changes slightly every year) to convert raw scores into composite scores grouped into broad AP grade categories. The weights for the multiple-choice sections are determined by the Chief Reader, who uses a process called *equating*. This process compares the current year's exam performance on selected multiple-choice questions to that of a previous year, establishing a level of achievement for the current year's group and a degree of difficulty for the current exam. This data is combined with historical trends and the reader's professional evaluation to determine the weights and tables.

The AP free-response is graded by teacher volunteers, grouped at scoring tables, and led by a chief faculty consultant. The consultant sets the grading scale that translates the raw score into the composite score. Past grading illustrations are available to teachers from the College Board, and may be ordered using the contact information given on page 3. These actual examples of student responses and a grade analysis can be

---

* Candidates' scores are weighted by a formula determined in advance each year by the AP Economics Development Committee.

of great assistance to both the student and the teacher as a learning or review tool.

Composite Score	AP Grade	Percentage of students at this grade (2000 Macro)
70 – 90	5 (extremely well qualified)	14.4
54 – 69	4 (well qualified)	28.6
45 – 53	3 (qualified)	16.8
29 – 44	2 (possibly qualified)	24.0
0 – 28	1 (no recommendation)	16.0

Total number of students: 23,581
Mean Grade: 3.01

STUDYING FOR YOUR AP EXAM

Use previous tests and quizzes to provide a study guide outline. Focus particular attention on questions that you got wrong. Take care not to repeat the same mistake.

Study with another student or in a group. Take turns asking each other questions. You will be amazed at how much you learn by playing the teacher!

For both Macroeconomics and Microeconomics, draw all the key models that you are required to be fluent in. Practice the possible movements that may result from change in the variables present in the model. For example, draw the AE model. Label all elements. How would the model react to an increase in government spending? Increase in taxes? Budget gap?

Create a study sheet with all of the key formulae (see Appendix B). Use the text or past exams to test your ability to solve questions on the money multiplier or price elasticity. Continue until you are error-free.

Prepare for the test over several days. Don't cram. Talk with your teacher regarding areas that you don't understand. Give your teacher adequate time to prepare an answer.

Whenever possible, take as many practice tests as possible. Review errors with your teacher or other students. Again, past tests and quizzes are invaluable as a learning tool.

TEST-TAKING TIPS

This test has time limits. Do not dwell on any one question. For the multiple-choice sections, do not spend more than one minute on a question. Come back to it later if time permits.

Be calm. If you have prepared properly, you are competent in the subject area and the test will prove it.

Immediately write key formulae and models on the test cover. This may save you from simple errors as time constraints pressure you. During the free-response sections, use part of the reading period for this.

Answer questions of a lower degree of difficulty first. The first time through, for example, complete definitions of scarcity or economic trade-offs. Circle the questions that require calculations or involve complicated reasoning, like trade equilibrium or FOMC manipulation of the business cycle.

Use the process of elimination when you are unsure of an answer. If you are unable to narrow a multiple-choice question to two possible right answers, move on. You will be penalized $1/4$ point for each wrong answer, but you will not lose any points for leaving it blank. However, do not overuse this method; leaving 15 or 20 questions blank is not advisable.

Assume no knowledge on the part of the test grader. For the free-response questions, writing as though the reader is unfamiliar with the subject will force you to answer more thoroughly.

Devote 25 minutes to the first free-response question in each section. The first question generally has more components, requires more information, and is worth 50% of the free-response total score. For each of the two remaining questions, allot $12^{1}/2$ minutes each.

Know the directions and format for each section of the exam. Familiarizing yourself with the directions and format of the different test sections will not only save you time, but will also ensure that you alleviate some uncertainty and its corresponding anxiety. For example, in the instructions to the free-response sections is a statement urging you to "emphasize the line of reasoning that generated your results; it is not enough to list the results of your analysis." This type of warning is very significant and might make a big difference in the way you approach this section.

Be prepared to draw and label any graphs necessary to a complete answering of free-response questions. Drawing the models will help you discover the correct answer. Most of the written answers are enhanced by reference to a model. Be neat, and clearly label all elements. If possible, link models together (e.g., AE to the AD/AS model, price to a purely competitive firm to price in a purely competitive industry, etc.).

Understand and answer the free-response questions employing the given structure (outline format) of the question. For the five-point structure, the first part (worth three points) may restate the topic and break down into three "impact" questions. The second part (worth 2 points) may be on a related topic, and have two additional variables. See the practice tests in this book for samples.

If you use an economic term, define it. If you give a conclusion, e.g., price increases, explain why the price rose—you need to.

When in doubt, go back to the basic market model, MB = MC. Most economic activity employs this equation in some measure. At the very least, it will never hurt you.

WHAT YOU'LL FACE ON TEST DAY

You will face two separate exams of 2 hours and 10 minutes in length, divided by a lunch break. Be sure to bring both #2 pencils and blue or black pens. No calculators are allowed. Be sure to read the test-taking tips before the exam.

▼

BASIC ECONOMIC CONCEPTS REVIEW

BASIC ECONOMIC CONCEPTS REVIEW

KEY TERMS:

- Scarcity
- Needs and Wants
- Origin of Economics
- Economic Choice
- Trade-offs
- PPF Curve
- Law of Diminishing Marginal Returns
- Law of Increasing Opportunity Cost
- Laws of Supply and Demand
- Determinants of Supply
- Law of Diminishing Marginal Utility
- Determinants of Demand
- Change in Quantity Supplied or Demanded
- Change in Supply or Demand
- Markets
- Equilibrium Price
- Shortage
- Surplus
- Productive Efficiency
- Allocative Efficiency
- Market Equilibrium

- Four Factors of Production (Inputs)
- Types of Economic Systems
- Circular Flow Model

ECONOMIC FOUNDATIONS

The study of economics involves a specific way of looking at how things work in the world. This approach has three main components: economic methods, macroeconomics, and microeconomics. Adam Smith is considered the "founding father" of economics, and his book, *The Wealth of Nations*, presented many of the concepts upon which this course is based. Since his work was published (in 1776), many others have furthered the study of economics, though they certainly have not always agreed with Smith. In fact, four general—and differing—viewpoints have evolved regarding the workings of markets: Classical, Keynesian, Monetary, and Neo-classical. These differing schools of thought are discussed in the macroeconomics review portion of this book.

Economics is always about limits. We are, by the very nature of our existence, limited to the resources provided by the planet. Our wants and needs, however, are not limited, and therein lies the rub! The result is scarcity, the fundamental reality of economics. Because of scarcity, humankind must engage in production choices. The primary decision asks: Which of our needs and wants do we satisfy, and which go unfulfilled? Answering this question forces people to make choices, and trade-offs result. Economists help us to understand these choices and the variety of possibilities that we face. Economists employ models that help us to focus on specific relationships that exist in the production and consumption of goods and services. These models employ the scientific method, in that they apply logical analysis based on economic principles to predict and explain outcomes, as well as suggest policies.

Another basic observation of economics is that the economic choices we make result in trade-offs that can be measured. As those trade-offs are measured, we realize that various combinations of goods and services can be produced. However, as we produce more of one good, we incur a cost, in the form of lost production of an alternative good or service. The PPF Curve, the Law of Diminishing Marginal Returns, and the Law of Increasing Opportunity Cost help us to understand this axiom. Together, these realities govern the behavior of the supplier in the free market system. Let's start our review with a look at the PPF Curve.

Production Possibilities Frontier Curve

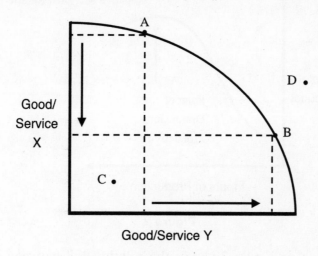

Figure 1

Figure 1 shows that as you move from point A to point B along the production curve, the quantity of Y produced increases, but the quantity of X decreases. In other words, you sacrifice X to gain Y. This is termed *opportunity cost*. The curve is bowed outward to represent the economic reality that as an input of production is used up, its output diminishes. The reverse of this procedure, a sacrifice of Y in order to produce more X, is possible as well. The curve represents the maximum possible combinations available. It is possible for an economy to produce inside the curve at C, a point that represents underusage of production inputs. The point of production represented by D is not possible given the current inputs (resources) present in the economy; to achieve D would require economic growth resulting from an increase in the inputs of production.

ORIGINS OF SUPPLY

Law of Diminishing Marginal Returns

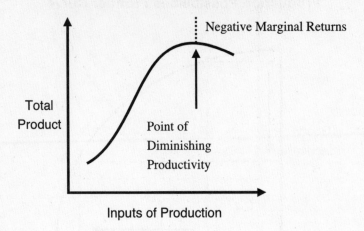

Figure 2

The model in figure 2 shows the relationship between the inputs of production and the total production resulting from those inputs. The inputs of production are: raw material, labor, capital (money or goods), and entrepreneurship. Initially, as we increase the factors of production, output increases at an increasing rate. At some point, however, additional inputs not only create output at a diminishing rate, but actually decrease the total output. The production table (table 1) demonstrates that relationship. Notice that as the third input is added to production, the total output increases from 12 to 16, but the marginal rate of change has decreased from 7 units gained to only 4 units of gained production. This is a diminishing rate, hence the name *Law of Diminishing Marginal Returns*. When the fifth input is added, the total productivity actually decreases from 16 to 12, a loss of 4 units.

Table 1

Input	1	2	3	4	5
Output	5	12	16	16	12

Law of Increasing Opportunity Costs

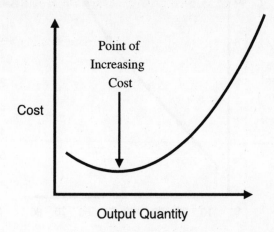

Figure 3

There is a clear relationship between the decrease in productivity and the increase in opportunity cost. As shown in figure 3, when productivity diminishes, the cost of production increases. This is what governs the law of supply and is why the graph slopes upward. A change in price causes movement along the supply curve. Why? Because a higher price covers the higher cost of increased production; more product is brought to market. Figure 4 shows this direct relationship.

Determinants of supply (that is, the prices of raw materials, labor, capital, and entrepreneurship) may cause the curve to shift (see figure 5). An increase in the price of the inputs of production causes a contraction in supply. This is shown as an upward and leftward movement of the supply curve. If input prices decrease, the supply curve moves downward and to the right, representing an overall increase in supply. Because the producer's cost of production begins to increase at some point, a producer must receive a higher sales price to be induced to make additional product. Remember, a producer is driven by profit, and maximum profit is the goal. Therefore, producers seek minimum cost per unit of production for the highest productive efficiency.

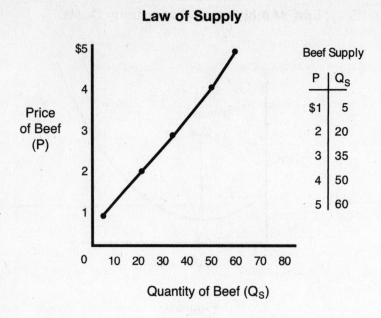

Figure 4

If the determinants of supply reduce the cost of production, the supply curve shifts from S_1 to S_2 (as shown in figure 5). This shift represents an overall increase in the quantity of goods brought to market at lower prices. If the determinants of supply increase the cost of production, the supply curve shifts from S_3 to S_1. This change in supply represents a decrease in the quantity of goods brought to market at higher prices.

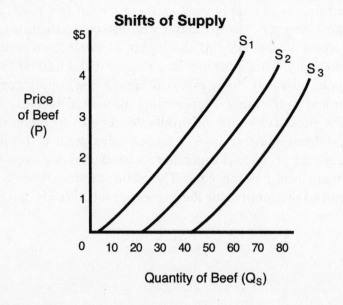

Figure 5

ORIGINS OF DEMAND

Increasing opportunity costs cause producers to behave in a predictable manner. Consumers also behave in a predictable manner because of scarcity. Consumers seek goods and services to satisfy their needs and wants. Though our needs and wants are unlimited, both the existence and the availability of the economic resources necessary to meet those needs are limited. Economic systems are developed to address this basic conflict. In a free market system, our income limits our ability to satisfy our desires (this is called the *rationing power* of prices). Economists believe that consumer satisfaction can be measured, since consumers attach a dollar value to goods and services (g/s). The more satisfaction derived from a g/s, the higher the price you are willing to pay. When we measure a group of consumers, we determine their demand schedule for a particular item. Price serves as a means of rationing the g/s produced.

Demand

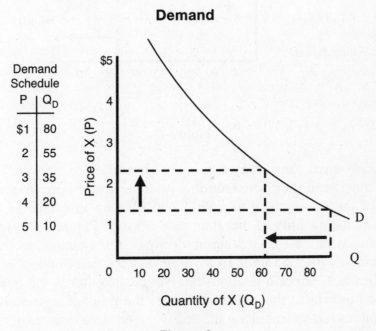

Demand Schedule

P	Q_D
$1	80
2	55
3	35
4	20
5	10

Quantity of X (Q_D)

Figure 6

Figure 6 is a graphic model of a demand table for good X. At a low price of $1, consumers are willing to buy 80 units; when the price rises to $2, consumers demand fewer units, 55. Notice that a change in price causes a change in the quantity demanded. The relationship between a change in price and a change in quantity demanded is a basic economic understanding. A primary feature of demand is that as price rises, the quantity demanded falls; and as price falls, the quantity demanded increases. Economists call this inverse relationship the *Law of Demand*. Why is this inverse relationship always present in consumer behavior? The primary answer stems from the nature of humankind, established in the law of diminishing marginal utility.

Diminishing Marginal Utility

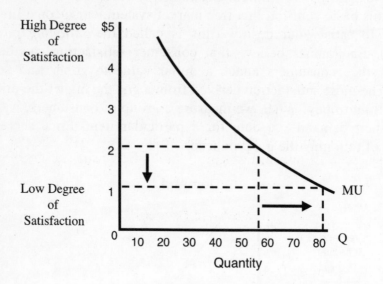

Figure 7

Economists can survey a group of consumers to measure the relationship between their satisfaction with a particular item (expressed in terms of the money they are willing to give up in exchange for that item) and the quantity of that item they possess. Figure 7 shows that as the quantity increases, satisfaction declines. For example, as the quantity increases from 55 units to 80 units, satisfaction diminishes from 2 to 1. This is an inverse relationship. Notice also that as the quantity of the good increases, the consumer values the product less; a change in price causes movement along the utility curve. As a consumer increases consumption of a good or service, the marginal utility obtained from each additional unit decreases. This principle, called the *Law of Diminishing Marginal Utility*, is what governs consumer behavior. The more of something I have, the less I value it. Consumers tell producers by their dollar expenditures the quantity of output they are willing to buy at various prices. To entice consumers to purchase increased quantity, producers must lower the price. This principle is the guiding hand behind the law of demand.

Finally, because consumer (sovereignty) demand may change at any time (figure 8), the entire schedule may shift outward (D_2 to D_3) signaling greater demand; or inward (D_2 to D_1), indicating less demand. These changes in demand are caused by a group of factors called the *determinants of demand*:

- Tastes and preferences

- Income

- Price and availability of substitute and complementary goods

- Future price or quantity expectations

- Number of buyers (population size)

- Government regulation

So, for example, if red shirts became trendy, the demand for red shirts would shift outward, resulting in higher prices and greater quantity bought.

Shifts in Demand

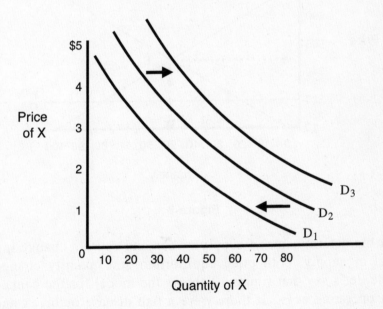

Quantity of X

Figure 8

MARKETS

The forces of supply and demand come together in the market-place. The market is a mechanism, a place where buyers and sellers of goods and services meet to satisfy their self-interest. The invisible forces of supply and demand interact to determine the price and quantity of goods bought and sold in the marketplace. The model portrayed in figure 9 assumes that competition is present for both producers and consumers. Free markets seek a balance between the interests of buyer and seller. This compromise point is known as the *equilibrium price*. It is the point at which supply and demand intersect. Equilibrium is significant, for it is at this price and quantity that the market clears, the price stabilizes, and product is available. Move from this price or quantity, and either shortage (inadequate supply of goods) or surplus (excess unsold goods) results. Economists have developed a graphic model of this event.

Market Equilibrium

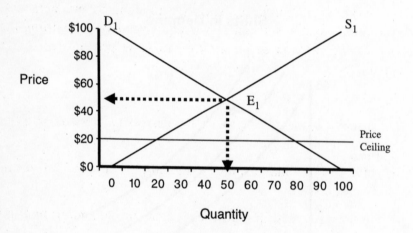

Figure 9

If the determinants of supply or demand cause a change in either demand or supply, both price equilibrium and quantity change. For example, let's say that figure 10 shows the model for the canned tuna market operating at E_1. If there were a fish disease outbreak and tuna became less available, the supply curve would shift inward, to the left, resulting in a higher equilibrium price of tuna and lower equilibrium quantity at E_2.

Tuna Market Equilibrium

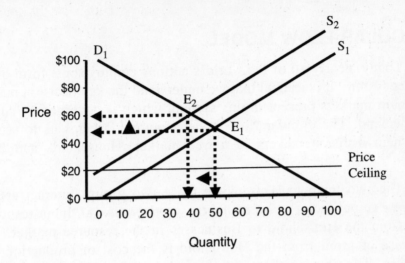

Figure 10

In markets, the forces of supply and demand are constantly at work. Economic systems organize society's decisions regarding the use of resources. Production of all goods and services requires four main resource inputs:

1. Land—raw materials.

2. Capital—means of production (investment goods) and finance capital (money used to acquire capital goods).

3. Labor—human resources, including both manual and intellectual skills.

4. Entrepreneurship—business organization and/or innovation.

Over the years, humankind has organized the means and distribution of production into four economic system types:

1. Free market—consumers and producers operate in an unregulated environment.

2. Traditional—society does not change its methods of production or consumption.

3. Command (state centrally planned)—government agencies regulate production and consumption.

4.   Mixed market—system blends free market, traditional, and state planning.

CIRCULAR FLOW MODEL

Today, nearly all of the world's nations employ some form of the market system. It is critical that we understand the key decision makers and main markets present in this system, which is governed by supply and demand. The circular flow model (figure 11) helps us to see the two main decision makers in a free market: Households and Businesses.

The two main markets where these two groups interact are the *resource* (input factor) *market* and the *product market*. Input resources flow from the Household to Businesses in the resource market. This purchase of input from the Household is the cost of production to a business. The sale of these resources by Households to Businesses generates Household income (wages, rents, interest, and profits). Remember, one of the key features of a free market economy is that the means (inputs) of production are owned by the individual. The product market is the place where Businesses sell their goods and services to Households. This sale to the Household is the source of a Business's revenue. When a Business subtracts its costs from this revenue, profit/loss is determined. This consumption of goods and services by Households is where the income earned from the resource market is expended. When a Household subtracts its consumption expenditures from its income, savings or debt are determined.

Circular Flow Model

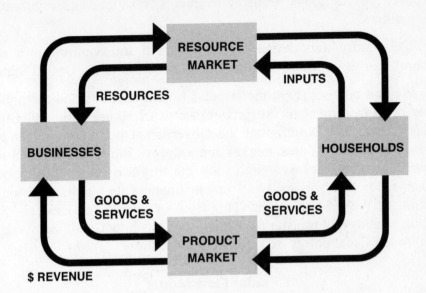

Figure 11

The United States has a mixed market economy, primarily employing free market principles. Among the most important characteristics of a market system are:

- private property
- freedom to enter or exit production markets
- freedom to dispose of your property as you see fit
- freedom to work in any area for which you are qualified
- freedom to buy goods and services that satisfy your wants
- freedom to act in your own self-interest
- competition among producers
- competition among consumers
- specialization/division of labor
- presence of a money system
- government provision of legal framework, enforcement, and infrastructure

This last point creates issues of market failure, spillover benefits and costs, public goods, transfer payments, taxation, and regulation, among others.

The nature and degree of government intervention into our economy causes constant, and often heated, debate in the United States.

We can now return to the circular flow model and add the public sector of Government to the private sector of Households and Businesses (figure 12). Notice that the Government purchases goods and services from the product market and employs input factors from the resource market. These purchases are the origin of our public goods, such as roads and bridges. Government finances its purchases through taxation of the private sector. This flow of goods, services, and tax dollars (subsidy and transfer payments) suggests how Government might try, through fiscal policy, to stabilize the economy.

Circular Flow Model

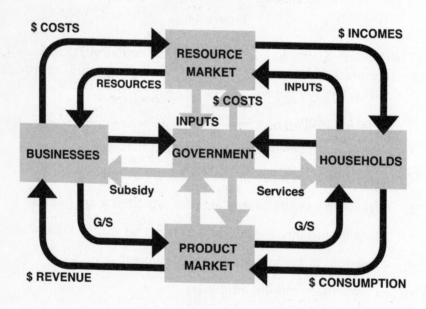

Figure 12

Today, the majority of the world's nations have agreed to follow many of these principles, and joined together in the World Trade Organization. This organization has contributed to increased specialization in the world, creating greater productive efficiency. Nations today seek absolute or comparative advantage in production, resulting in greater trade and thus increasing their standard of living. This freer international trade has greatly increased global competition, which affects a large number of U.S. firms. The supporters and critics of free trade continue to debate the advantages and disadvantages of this mixed market system. Nonetheless, imports and exports play a role in our economy. Imports and exports are the final link in the chain that forms our economy (figure 13). To see this, we return to the circular flow model for a last time.

Circular Flow Model

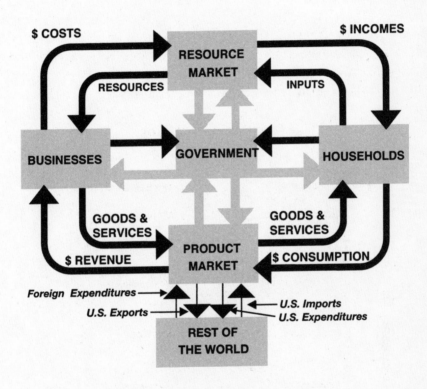

Figure 13

Notice that when the United States exports goods and services to the rest of the world, wealth from those other nations flows into ours. The opposite is also true: when we purchase foreign goods and services (import), our wealth flows into the foreign producer. This forms the basis for the balance of trade (examined in greater detail later). Essentially, exports add to our wealth (favorable balance of trade) while imports subtract from our wealth (unfavorable balance of trade). Also note that imports increase goods and services available for domestic consumption.

MICROECONOMICS
REVIEW

AP MICROECONOMICS COURSE STRUCTURE

MICROECONOMICS: BASIC ECONOMIC CONCEPTS

The study of microeconomics requires students to understand that, in any economy, the existence of limited resources and unlimited wants results in the need to make choices. An effective AP course begins by studying the concepts of opportunity costs and trade-offs, which can be illustrated by the production possibilities curve or other analytical examples. The course can then proceed to a consideration of how different types of economies determine which goods and services to produce, how to produce them, and to whom to distribute them.

It is also important that students understand why and how specialization and exchange increase the total output of goods and services. In this context, students need to be able to differentiate between absolute and comparative advantage; to identify comparative advantage from differences in output levels and labor costs; and to determine the basis on which mutually advantageous trade can take place between countries. Specific examples from actual economic situations can be used to illustrate and reinforce the principles involved.

THE NATURE AND FUNCTIONS OF PRODUCT MARKETS

The study of the nature and functions of product markets covers three broad areas.

THE INTERACTION OF MARKET SUPPLY AND DEMAND

A well-planned AP course requires an analysis of the determinants of supply and demand and the ways in which changes in these determinants affect supply and demand curves. In particular, the course helps students make the important distinction between movements along the curves and shifts in the curves themselves. The course should also emphasize the process by which equilibrium price and quantity are determined and the impact of government policies such as price floors and ceilings, excise taxes, tariffs, and quotas.

THE THEORY OF CONSUMER CHOICE

Students should learn that consumers choose goods in the market to maximize satisfaction. By examining the demand side of the product market, students learn how incomes, prices, and tastes affect consumer purchases. Here it is important that students gain an understanding of how the income and substitution effects determine the shape of the demand curve, how an individual's demand curve is derived, and how the individual and market demand curves are related. Students are also expected to study the characteristics that determine the price elasticity of demand and to apply the concept of elasticity to the analysis of real-world problems.

THE SUPPLY SIDE OF THE PRODUCT MARKET

By examining the theory of the firm, the course introduces discussion of a firm's economic costs. This discussion includes an analysis of the relationship between diminishing returns and marginal costs; the relationships between total, average, and marginal costs in the long run and in the short run; and the behavior of firms in different types of market structures. In its discussion of perfect competition, the course focuses on determining short-run and long-run equilibria, both for the profit-maximizing individual firm and for the industry; and on the equilibrium relationships between price, marginal and average revenues, marginal and average costs, and profits. In considering the market behavior of a monopolist, students compare a monopolist's price, level of output, and profit with those of a firm operating in a perfectly competitive market. By paying particular attention to the concept of allocative efficiency, students learn how and why competitive firms achieve an efficient allocation of resources, whereas monopolists do not. Students also learn why government should in some cases encourage competition and in others allow a regulated monopoly to exist. Lastly, well-prepared students will gain some familiarity with the characteristics of monopolistic competition and oligopoly and their effects on efficiency.

FACTOR MARKETS

In the course section on factor markets, students learn that the concepts of supply and demand apply to markets for factors such as land, labor, and capital, as well as to product markets. Students analyze the concept of derived demand, examine the relationship of the demand for a factor to the factor's marginal product, and consider the role of factor prices in the allocation of scarce resources. When the markets for different factors are considered separately, students generally give most attention to the labor market, particularly labor supply, and wage and employment determination. Although the course may emphasize perfectly competitive labor markets, the effect of deviations from perfect competition (such as minimum wages, unions, and product market monopolies) can be considered. For the factors of land and capital, students might examine the concept of economic rent and the relationship of the interest rate to the supply of and demand for investment funds. By studying the determination of factor prices, students gain an understanding of the sources of income inequality in a market economy.

EFFICIENCY, EQUITY, AND THE ROLE OF GOVERNMENT

It is important for students to understand the arguments for and against government intervention in an otherwise competitive market. Students examine the conditions for economic efficiency and the ways in which public goods and externalities generate market failures even in perfectly competitive economies. In addition, students are expected to study the effectiveness of government policies that are designed to correct market failures, such as subsidies, taxes, quantity controls, and public provision of goods and services. Although there is no generally accepted standard for judging the equity of an economy's income distribution, a well-designed course will examine the impact of government tax policies and transfer programs on the distribution of income and on economic efficiency.

MICROECONOMICS REVIEW

KEY TERMS:

- Price elasticiy
  - Elastic
  - Inelastic
- Total revenue and elasticity
- Cross elasticity of demand
- Cross elasticity of income
- Price ceiling
- Price floor
- Price elasticity of supply
- Consumer utility maximization and budget income limits
- Explicit cost
- Implicit cost
- Short run
- Long run
- TFC, TVC, AFC, AVC, ATC, MC
- Economy of scale
- Least cost (output and input analysis)
- Maximum Profit (Output and Input analysis)
- Four market models:
  - Pure competition
  - Monopoly (imperfect competition)
  - Monopolistic competition
  - Oligopoly (shared monopoly)
- Cartel
- Marginal product
- Marginal revenue product
- Marginal resource cost
- Monopsony
- Union effect
- Minimum wage
- Lorenz curve

- Taxation
  - Progressive
  - Proportional
  - Regressive
- Transfer payment
- Public goods
- Spillover cost and benefit
- Merger
  - Horizontal
  - Vertical
  - Conglomerate

INTERACTION OF SUPPLY AND DEMAND

As we learned in the initial general review, economics is always about limits. Resources are limited, whereas our wants and needs are unlimited. The result is scarcity, which forces us to make consumption and production choices. Various combinations of goods and services (g/s) can be produced. However, as we produce more of one g/s, we incur a cost in the form of lost production of an alternative good or service. These forces underlie the laws of demand and supply. In microeconomics we will extend our investigation of those forces. Let's start our review with a look at the impact of changes in price on the buyers and sellers of a g/s. This is called *price elasticity*.

PRICE ELASTICITY OF DEMAND

We already know that consumers are governed by the law of diminishing marginal utility. Thus, they will buy more of a g/s only if its price declines. Elasticity gives us a quantitative means by which to measure this consumer sensitivity to price change. The simple test for elasticity gives us the formula:

$$E_d = \frac{\% \text{ change in quantity demanded of g/s A}}{\% \text{ change in price of g/s A}}$$

This calculation yields a percentage outcome that allows us to compare consumer behavior across product types and prices. Economists use the following benchmarks to classify the nature of the price elasticity quotient:

- If $E_d > 1$, then demand is elastic.

- If $E_d < 1$, then demand is inelastic.

- If $E_d = 1$, the demand is unitary elastic.

The minus or plus sign of the change is irrelevant, as we are concerned only with the amount of change, not whether it is an increase or a decrease. For example, let's say that the price of a soft drink increased by 20% and the demand changed by 40%.

$E_d = 0.40/0.20 = 2 > 1$, therefore demand is elastic

This demand is classified as elastic or flexible because consumers showed greater sensitivity to price than to quantity of product demanded. In other words, the consumer was more concerned with the price than with the g/s. If consumers behaved in the opposite manner, we would consider their demand to be inelastic or inflexible.

$E_d = 0.20/0.40 = 0.5 < 1$, therefore demand is inelastic

In this case, consumers have demonstrated a greater concern for the product than for the price. Without question, producers of g/s are very interested in customers' reaction to price changes. Remember, the consumer (sovereignty) is king.

Unitary elasticity occurs when the consumer is equally concerned with price and product. Unitary elasticity is demonstrated as:

$E_d = 0.50/0.50 = 1$, therefore demand is unitary elastic

Extreme cases of consumer reaction to price are termed *perfectly inelastic* if the price coefficient is near zero. This represents a g/s that is so needed by the consumer that it is a necessity for life, such as insulin to a diabetic. This is drawn as a line perpendicular to the horizontal axis (figure 1).

Perfectly Inelastic Demand

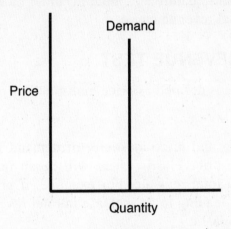

Figure 1

The other extreme case of consumer reaction to price is called *perfectly elastic*, if the price coefficient is significantly greater than 1. This represents a g/s that is completely unnecessary to the consumer— a luxury. This is drawn as a line perpendicular to the vertical axis (figure 2).

Perfectly Elastic Demand

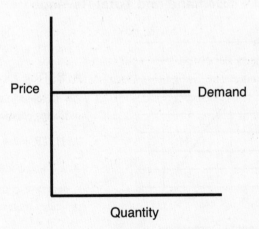

Figure 2

One of the limitations of the simple test for elasticity is that, depending on which portion of a demand curve you measure, the outcome coefficient will be elastic in the upper left portion and inelastic in the lower right half. Calculating the slope of the demand curve could also be misleading, as you would be measuring absolute change over the entire demand for the product. Elasticity, in contrast, seeks relative changes in price and quantity. A more accurate measure of consumer elasticity is the total revenue curve.

THE TOTAL REVENUE TEST

Total revenue is defined as price multiplied by quantity:

$$TR = P \times Q$$

Total revenue and price elasticity of demand are related. If demand is relatively price elastic, there will be an inverse relationship between price and total revenue. For example, if price decreases and demand increases, leading to an increase in total revenue, then demand is relatively price elastic.

Conversely, a direct relationship exists between price and total revenue when demand is relatively price inelastic. For example, an increase in price leading to an increase in total revenue, or a decrease in price leading to a decrease in total revenue, generates a price inelastic demand curve.

The impact of the total revenue test is best viewed graphically (figure 3).

Demand and Total Revenue

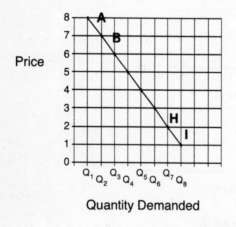

- At A, TR = 8 × 1 = $8
- At B, TR = 7 × 2 = $14
- An increase in total revenue indicates elasticity of demand.
- At H, TR = 2 × 7 = $14
- At I, TR = 1 × 8 = $8
- A decrease in total revenue indicates inelasticity of demand.

Figure 3

This method of measuring consumer reaction to price changes is most useful when the results are plotted to show the changes in a firm's total revenue. Notice that at some point, the sale of one more good is detrimental to the firm's total revenue, because to sell that good, the firm has to lower the price so much that the total revenue actually declines. Why would a firm want to sell that extra good if it will lose revenue by making the sale? It won't. Firms want to maximize profit.

Price Elasticity and Total Revenue Curve

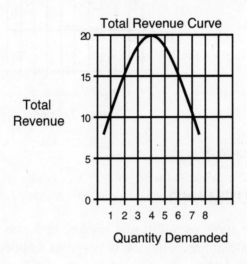

- This allows us to see that there is indeed a maximum revenue point.
- Selling more product beyond Q4 actually decreases revenues and thus profits.

Figure 4

When the fourth unit is sold, total revenue is maximized. If the fifth unit is sold, total revenue declines.

In figure 5, we align the demand curve from figure 3 with the total revenue curve from figure 4. The different ranges of elasticity become clear when we employ the total revenue test to find the elastic and inelastic portions of the demand curve.

Demand and Total Revenue

Total Revenue Curve

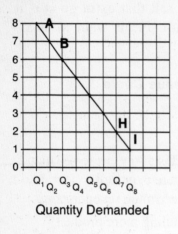

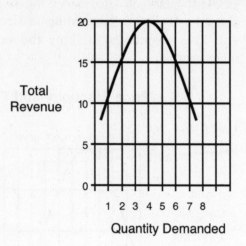

Figure 5

CROSS ELASTICITY OF DEMAND

The cross elasticity formula gives us additional insight into consumer behavior. This aspect of consumer behavior is of great importance to producers in determining what quantity of g/s to produce. Sellers anticipate the impact of price changes on the quantity demand of a g/s by gauging the effect on the total revenue the firm will generate. Cross elasticity (denoted as E_{ab}) also builds on the concepts of substitute and complementary g/s. The formula is:

$$E_{ab} = \frac{\%\ of\ change\ in\ the\ Q_d\ of\ g/s\ A}{\%\ of\ change\ in\ the\ price\ of\ g/s\ A}$$

If the quotient is positive, then the g/s are substitutes for each other. For example, if Jiffy peanut butter increases in price and the sale of Peter Pan peanut butter increases, then consumers have reacted to the increase in the price of Jiffy by changing to Peter Pan.

If the coefficient is negative, the products are used together and are complements to each other. If ice cream increases in price and the quantity of fudge topping demanded decreases, the price of one has affected the demand for the other. If the goods are unrelated, a zero or near-zero outcome results.

Income elasticity of demand determines and classifies the relationship between income and demand for a g/s. The formula for income elasticity of demand is:

$$E_{income} = \frac{\% \text{ of change in the quantity demanded}}{\% \text{ of change in income}}$$

If the outcome is positive, then an increase in income has resulted in an increase in the quantity demanded. This indicates that the g/s is normal or superior (brand-name).

If the outcome is negative, then a decrease in income has increased the purchase of the g/s. This is an inferior g/s, for as income increases people tend to buy less of an inferior g/s (generic label). However, as income decreases, people tend to be forced, by income budget constraints, to buy more of an inferior g/s. This helps explain why consumers, during a recession, continue to buy staples, such as food, but forgo durable goods such as electronics or automobiles.

GOVERNMENT INTERVENTION IN THE FREE MARKET

If the general public, lobbyists, and government conclude that a g/s is over/underpriced or over/undersupplied, the government may alter the market structure to encourage or discourage price and quantity changes. This can be accomplished through either a price ceiling or a price floor.

PRICE CEILING

A government price ceiling is a declaration that the price charged by suppliers is too high. Therefore, the government legislates a price cap. Producers cannot by law charge a price higher than that set by government. This maximum price may appear attractive to consumers if it applies to items like rent or food staples, like sugar during wartime. A supply and demand model helps to illustrate the issue. Let's use rent control for a one-bedroom apartment as an example.

Government Interference: Price Ceiling

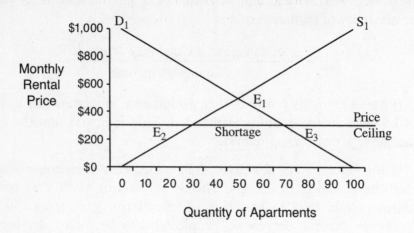

Figure 6

The government price ceiling depicted in figure 6 shows the effect that a cap on price has on the marketplace. Equilibrium price for the apartment would be $300 and equilibrium supply is 40,000 units. The government then mandates a rent control ceiling of $100 to landlords. This new forced price will cause a swelling of demand for these apartments to 60,000 units. However, landlords will supply only 20,000 units at this price. Where do the apartment units go? If profit is not present, firms will flee the market. Perhaps they convert the apartments into condominiums or office space, which are markets free from government control. Many other negative externalities may occur, such as the formation of a black market, poor quality of remaining apartments, higher prices for similar goods, and diversion of investment from housing.

PRICE FLOORS

A government price floor is a declaration that the price paid by consumers is too low. This results in production levels that may deprive some consumers of the g/s. Therefore, the government legislates a price minimum. This new price minimum, set above equilibrium, will stimulate production, as new profit levels are guaranteed to producers. Consumers cannot by law pay a price lower than that set by the government. This higher minimum price (especially for items such as food staples) is often justified by the realization of other societal benefits, such as maintenance of family farm ownership. If government intervention is predicated on a socioeconomic premise that overproduction of this g/s has spillover benefits, higher prices or subsidy of production are supported. A supply and demand model helps to illustrate the issue. Let's use milk production as an example (figure 7).

Government Interference: Price Floor

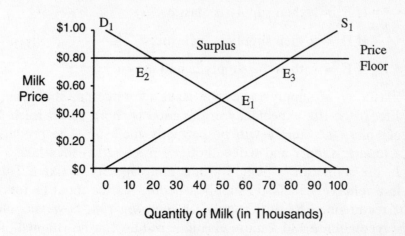

Figure 7

Assume that the free-market price for milk is $0.50 per quart and that 50,000 quarts are purchased each day. Government supports a new minimum price of $0.80 for producers. This new, higher price will stimulate suppliers to supply 80,000 quarts of milk daily. However, the higher price also causes the quantity demanded by consumers to fall to 20,000 quarts. This new minimum price results in a surplus of 60,000 quarts of milk. The dilemma now facing the government is how to dispose of the surplus milk. Should the good be transferred to the poor? Should it be destroyed? Should the government simply pay for nonproduction? The new, higher price disrupts the rationing effect of the free market. Allocative and productive efficiency are destroyed. For this reason, most economists generally oppose government interference in free markets.

PRICE ELASTICITY OF SUPPLY

We already know that producers are governed by the law of increasing opportunity cost (because they seek maximum profit or least loss). Thus, they will supply one more unit of good only if the sale price rises enough to cover the increased cost of production. The formula to determine elasticity of supply is basically the same as for demand.

$$E_s = \frac{\% \text{ of change in the } Q_s \text{ of g/s}}{\% \text{ of change in the price of g/s}}$$

Economists use the following benchmarks to classify the degree of elasticity present for the g/s:

- If $E_s > 1$, then supply is elastic.

- If $E_s < 1$, then supply is inelastic.

- If $E_s = 1$, then the supply is unit elastic.

Elasticity of supply raises the issue of long run, short run, and shelf life. If the life expectancy of the good is short, as for fresh fruits or vegetables, the supply will be perfectly inelastic. The producer is unable to alter supply and will sell at any price rather than take a total loss. In the short run, a plant's production capacity is fixed. This results in a relatively inelastic supply schedule, as the input factors cannot be recombined to shift supply. In the long run, however, factors can be recombined and a more elastic schedule can be attained. There is no total revenue test for elasticity of supply, as price and total revenue move in the same direction. The models depicting short-run inelastic supply and long-run elastic supply are shown in figure 8.

Elastic (Long-Run) and Inelastic (Short-Run) Supply

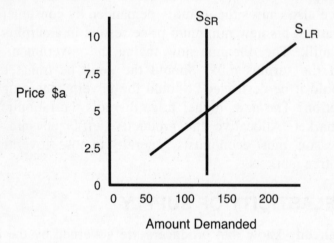

Figure 8

CONSUMER CHOICE

How do consumers choose goods and services in the market-place? What effect does a change in income have on consumer behavior? For the most part, the laws of demand, price elasticity, and cross elasticity (already reviewed conceptually) answer these two questions. Remember that the law of demand is based on the law of diminishing marginal utility. Quantitative analysis, however, is both helpful and revealing. An algebraic statement helps us view the decision-making process from a utility maximization standpoint. Consumers want to allocate their disposable income in such a way that they balance the last dollar spent on a product with its utility yield. This process of utility maximization, in its simplest form, begins with allocation of consumer dollars between two products. The formula is:

$$\frac{\text{Marginal Utility of Product X}}{\text{Price of X}} = \frac{\text{Marginal Utility of Product Y}}{\text{Price of Y}}$$

When limited income and set prices are brought into play, the consumer will allocate income in such a way as to balance marginal utility per dollar for every good purchased, and will spend all income (we assume no borrowing or savings at this time). The maximum utility per dollar within an income limit modifies the formula as follows:

$$\frac{\text{Marginal Utility of Product X}}{\text{Price of X}} = \frac{\text{Marginal Utility of Product Y}}{\text{Price of Y}}$$

= Income Limit

Table 1 provides an illustration of this behavior. Notice that marginal utility (Mu) per dollar is equal at several different combinations: 1A + 4B (5Mu per $), 2A + 5B (4Mu per $), and 3A + 6B (3Mu per $). Only the 2A + 5B combination maximizes our Mu per dollar and income limit of $9. Note that 1A + 4B = $6 underutilizes income, 2A + 5B = $9 meets the budget, and 3A + 3B = $12 exceeds the budget. If our income, utility of product, or prices changed, so too would our mix of goods. If the number of g/s increased, the formula would still apply and a balance of Mu and income would still be sought. Consumers allocate their income in such a way that the marginal utilities per dollar of expenditure on the last unit of each g/s purchased are as nearly equal as possible. This point expresses consumer equilibrium; the consumer will not stray from this balance unless stimulated to do so.

Table 1

Units of Product A ($2)	Marginal Utility of A	Marginal Utility per Dollar	Units of Product B ($1)	Marginal Utility of B	Marginal Utility per Dollar
1	10	5	1	8	8
2	8	4	2	7	7
3	6	3	3	6	6
4	4	2	4	5	5
5	3	1.5	5	4	4
6	2	1	6	3	3

INCOME CONSTRAINTS AND BUDGET LIMITS

Income limits lead to budget analysis, which is another way to explain consumer choice and works along with the concept of marginal utility. The budget line itself displays the various combinations of g/s that a consumer is willing and able to buy at a particular income. A budget line is necessary to reveal the consumer's income level/budget. Any combination inward of the budget line is attainable; any area outside the budget line is unattainable (unless income increases). The consumer combination of goods is possible anywhere along the income limit line. In figure 9, points A (4 units of B, 1 unit of A) and B (4 units of A, 1 unit of B) represent two possible combinations of goods that meet budget limits.

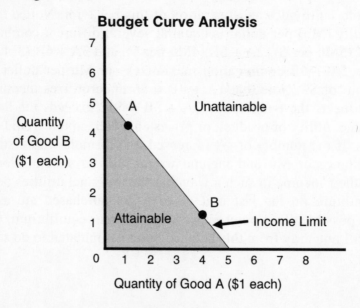

Budget Curve Analysis

Figure 9

If the income of the consumer or the price of the good changes, the budget line must be redrawn. For example, if the price of good B were reduced to $0.50, the new budget line would be as depicted in figure 10. Now the consumer can afford greater quantities at both point A (8 units of B and 1 of A) and point B (2 units of B and 4 units of A).

Budget Curve Analysis

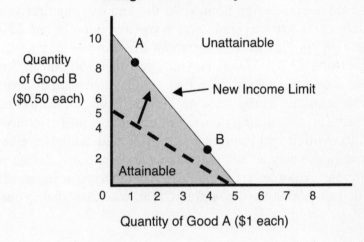

Figure 10

PRODUCER BEHAVIOR

Producer behavior is governed by self-interest. Producers seek maximum profit as their primary goal. Necessary to the understanding of a firm's profit is an awareness of the costs of production, consumer demand, revenue received, and competition present in the marketplace. Remember the circular flow model from figure 11 in the general review. A firm's decisions are based on the changing relationship between cost and revenue over different quantities of goods sold at various prices.

OPPORTUNITY (ECONOMIC) COST

Remember the concept of opportunity cost discussed at the beginning of this review. The more of an input employed by a firm in the production of a g/s, the greater the firm's cost in lost opportunity to produce an alternative g/s. Also, recall how the Law of Diminishing Marginal Returns (Marginal Productivity) explains the rising costs that occur at some point in the production schedule. Economists view economic cost in two ways, explicit and implicit costs. *Explicit (obvious) costs* are payments made to input resource suppliers. *Implicit (hidden) costs* are the lost opportunity of entrepreneurial talent and capital resources that were applied elsewhere. For example, suppose you are employed at a job that pays you $100,000 per year to design houses for a large construction firm. You decide to quit this job and start your own firm to custom-design homes. At the end of your first year, when all explicit costs are covered, you have a remainder of $50,000 of accounting profit. However, what about the forgone income from your previous efforts of $100,000? Haven't you lost $50,000 of former income? An economist would state that you have not had a normal profit unless you account for the forgone income from your previous job as an entrepreneurial (implicit) cost. So, economic profit is any amount above your explicit and implicit costs combined. This is a clear difference between the way an accountant and an economist define profit. In this particular example, an economist would say you incurred an economic loss of $50,000 (the amount that was less than your former salary).

PRODUCER TIME CONSTRAINTS

Demand for a firm's g/s can change quickly. A producer can be called upon by consumers to increase or decrease its production quantity at a moment's notice. Its profitability may depend on the time frame necessary to alter its inputs of production. Economists classify time into two key categories, short run and long run. Short run is a time period during which plant capacity to produce is said to be fixed or unchangeable. The inputs of production cannot be altered beyond a 24-hour-a-day, 7-day work week maximum. Long run is a time period during which plant capacity to produce is said to be changeable. All inputs of production can be altered, plants can be built or closed, and inputs can be added or reduced. Firms may enter or exit the industry altogether. No fixed amount of time defines short run or long run; it varies from industry to industry. Therefore, we see a difference in firms' short-run and long-run cost curves.

SHORT-RUN PRODUCTION COSTS

A firm must calculate all its costs of production before it can determine its profit/loss. First, a firm must pay for its input resources. These costs, which increase at some point, are variable costs (such as labor, energy, raw materials) that change at various levels of production. Firms also incur set costs. These fixed costs (such as rents, interest on debt, lost value of capital goods over time, insurance) must be paid regardless of whether a firm produces. When all these costs are added, we have a producer's total costs. Managers view the distinction between fixed and variable costs as significant, in that variable costs can be altered in the short run whereas fixed costs cannot. A firm that is unable to cover its variable costs must eventually shut down (unpaid workers will at some point seek employment elsewhere). Shut-down point is demonstrated graphically in figure 11.

Purely Competitive Firm

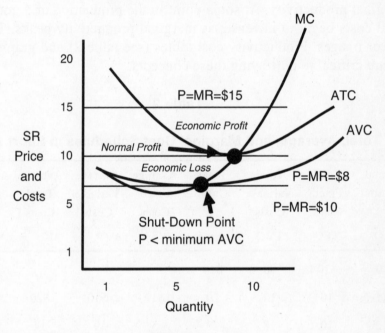

Figure 11

COST ANALYSIS

Producers are very interested in costs, as they are somewhat within the producers' control and determine a firm's very existence. Unit cost data, as depicted in figure 11, is meaningful in determining prices that must be charged at various levels of production to realize loss, normal, and economic profit points. Average fixed cost (AFC = TFC/Q), when plotted, shows that a firm's fixed costs decrease the most in the early stages of production quantity increase; even though a firm's fixed costs continuously decline, the rate of decline diminishes significantly. Average variable cost (AVC = TVC/Q) incorporates the law of diminishing returns: initial gains in productivity slow, opportunity costs rise, and average variable costs eventually increase. Average fixed cost and average variable cost, when added, give us the average total cost (ATC = AFC + AVC). Critical to a firm's decision to increase or decrease production is the concept of marginal cost. Marginal cost—the cost incurred by the last unit produced—is within a manager's control. Average cost figures do not give a manager the same specific information. Marginal cost is the additional cost of producing one more unit (MC = change in Total Cost / change in Quantity). Marginal cost is shaped by the same economic forces that shape average variable cost; that is, marginal productivity. At some point in the production of a good, marginal costs begin to increase, as marginal productivity peaks. They are mirror images. Productivity cost tables (see table 2) and graphic models are critical to portraying these concepts.

Table 2

Total, Average, and Marginal Cost Schedules in Short Run

Total Output	Total Fixed Costs	Total Variable Costs	Total Costs	Average Fixed Costs	Average Variable Costs	Average Total Costs	Marginal Costs
Q	TFC	TVC	TC=TFC+TVC	$AFC = \frac{TFC}{Q}$	$AVC = \frac{TVC}{Q}$	$ATC = \frac{TC}{Q}$	$MC = \frac{\Delta TC}{\Delta Q}$
0	$10	$0	$10				
1	10	10	20	$10	$10	$20	$10
2	10	18	28	5	9	14	8
3	10	25	35	3.33	8.33	11.6	7
4	10	30	40	2.5	7.5	10	5
5	10	35	45	2	7	9	5
6	10	42	52	1.66	7	8.66	7
7	10	50.6	60.6	1.44	7.2	8.6	8.6
8	10	60	70	1.25	7.5	8.75	9.4
9	10	80	90	1.1	8.8	10	20

- Note that AFC declines at a greater rate in the early stages of production.

- Note that AVC begins to increase after the sixth unit (diminishing marginal productivity).

- Note that ATC also increases after the seventh unit (cost decreases from AFC have a lesser impact than increases in AVC).

- Note that MC increases after the fifth unit of output.

The cost relationships expressed in table form can also be charted graphically, as in figure 12.

Firm Cost Curve

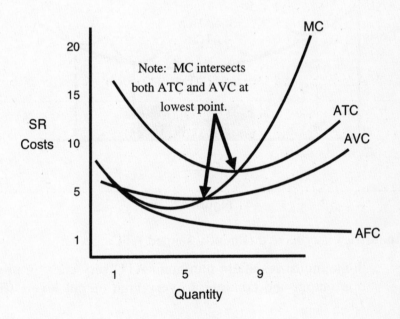

Figure 12

LONG-RUN COSTS OF PRODUCTION

Long run is a time frame in which firms can alter all inputs of production. Also, other firms can enter or exit production in the long run, thereby increasing or decreasing industry output. Long-run cost curves are made up of segments of short-run ATC curves (see figure

13). Each short-run cost curve has a minimum ATC point; long-run cost curves connect the ATC curves' minimums. The long-run cost curves reveal the concept of economies of scale. Some industries (usually for durable goods) do not attain minimum ATC until a fairly high output level is attained. The auto industry is a prime example. However, there is still a limit to the cost savings obtainable by increasing scale, and eventually factors such as bureaucracy of management, worker alienation, and government regulation will cause costs to increase (diseconomies of scale).

Long-Run Cost Curve Economy of Scale

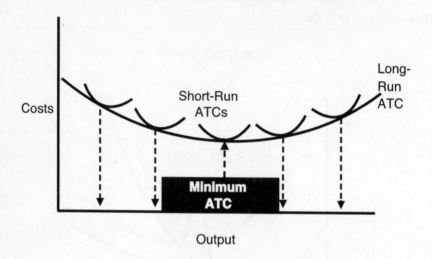

Figure 13

Industries may have differently shaped ATC curves:

- Some industries attain minimum ATC very early in production output and continue to very high output levels (figure 14).

Economies of Scale Long-Run ATC

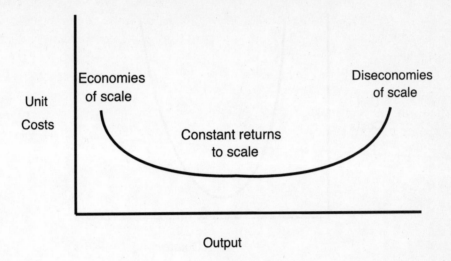

Output

Figure 14

- Some industries do not attain minimum ATC until they reach very high levels of output (figure 15).

Economies of Scale Long-Run ATC

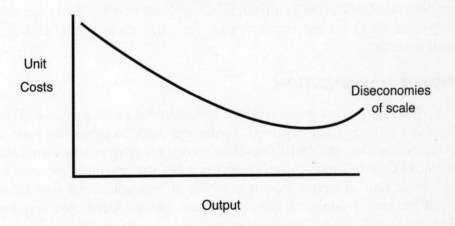

Output

Figure 15

- Some industries attain minimum ATC very early in output, but also reach diseconomies of scale very quickly (figure 16).

Economies of Scale Long-Run ATC

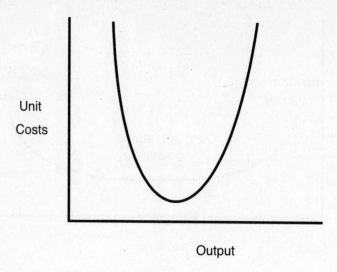

Figure 16

FOUR PRODUCTION MARKET MODELS

Economists group industries into four market types, based on the degree of competition present, ease of entrance or exit, and level of product standardization or differentiation. Note that the short-run cost curves of all firms are similar; what separates them is the nature of their revenue.

PROFIT MAXIMIZATION

All four market types seek the greatest total profit possible (Total Revenue – Total Cost = profit). Firms also seek to minimize loss; as discussed earlier, they will shut down when revenue is less than minimum AVC. Profit maximization occurs when the revenue generated by one more unit of output equals the cost of that additional unit (Marginal Revenue = Marginal Cost rule), and that marginal cost is rising. This rule applies to all four market models.

PERFECT COMPETITION MARKET MODEL

The perfect competition model has four distinct characteristics:

1. Many buyers and sellers; firms are price takers, unable to influence the prices they must charge.

2. Homogenous product; each firm makes an identical product and consumers make purchases based on price comparison only.

3. Freedom of exit and entry; no barriers limit a firm's behavior.

4. Perfect information; each buyer and seller is fully informed and rational.

These assumptions allow us to draw the purely competitive firm's revenue as perfectly elastic. Although the entire market for this g/s does have a demand curve (see figure 19), we are looking at an individual firm (table 3, figure 17) within an industry. The entire industry could act together to influence price, but one firm independently could not. A single firm has no pricing power. That is why economists call firms in a perfectly competitive market "price takers." Let's revisit the table of costs we dealt with earlier and add a revenue column.

Table 3

Total, Average, and Marginal Cost Schedules in Short Run

Total Output	Total Revenue	Total Costs	Average Fixed Costs	Average Variable Costs	Average Total Costs	Marginal Costs	Marginal Revenue = Price	Total Economic Profit+Loss
Q	TR = Price × Quantity	TC = TFC+TVC	$AFC = \frac{TFC}{Q}$	$AVC = \frac{TVC}{Q}$	$ATC = \frac{TC}{Q}$	$MC = \frac{\Delta TC}{\Delta Q}$	$MR = \frac{\Delta TR}{\Delta Q}$	TR–TC= Profit
0	0	$10						–10
1	10	20	$10	$10	$20	$10	$10	–10
2	20	28	5	9	14	8	10	–8
3	30	35	3.33	8.33	11.6	7	10	–5
4	40	40	2.5	7.5	10	5	10	0
5	50	45	2	7	9	5	10	+5
6	60	52	1.66	7	8.66	7	10	+8
7	70	60.6	1.44	7.2	8.6	8.6	10	+9.4
8	80	70	1.25	7.5	8.75	9.4	10	+10
9	90	90	1.1	8.8	10	20	10	0

Profit maximization occurs at the eighth unit of output when MR = MC and MC is rising. This profit maximization point is confirmed graphically as well.

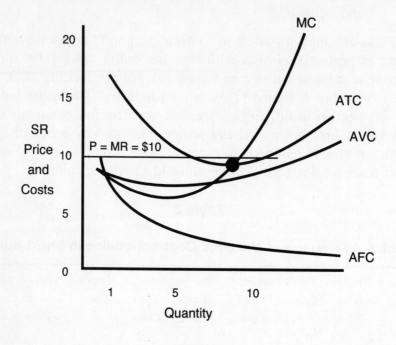

Individual Firm in Purely Competitive Market: Short-Run Economic Profit

Figure 17

This firm is enjoying an economic profit, as the MR = MC is above minimum ATC. What would happen if the price fell to $8? Let's return to the table (see table 4).

Table 4

Total, Average, and Marginal Cost Schedules in Short Run

Total Output	Total Revenue	Total Costs	Average Fixed Costs	Average Variable Costs	Average Total Costs	Marginal Costs	Marginal Revenue = Price	Total Economic Profit+Loss
Q	TR = Price × Quantity	TC = TFC+TVC	$AFC = \dfrac{TFC}{Q}$	$AVC = \dfrac{TVC}{Q}$	$ATC = \dfrac{TC}{Q}$	$MC = \dfrac{\Delta TC}{\Delta Q}$	$MR = \dfrac{\Delta TR}{\Delta Q}$	TR–TC= Profit
0	0	$10						−10
1	8	20	$10	$10	$20	$10	$8	−12
2	16	28	5	9	14	8	8	−12
3	24	35	3.33	8.33	11.6	7	8	−11
4	34	40	2.5	7.5	10	5	8	−6
5	40	45	2	7	9	5	8	−5
6	48	52	1.66	7	8.66	7	8	−4
7	56	60.6	1.44	7.2	8.6	8.6	8	−4.6
8	64	70	1.25	7.5	8.75	9.4	8	−6
9	72	90	1.1	8.8	10	20	8	−18

The MR = MC intersection occurs at 6 units of output. The firm is losing $4 at this level, but notice that this is its minimal loss. Firms experiencing a loss will attempt to minimize loss and will not shut down as long as they are covering minimum AVC. This situation is shown in figure 18.

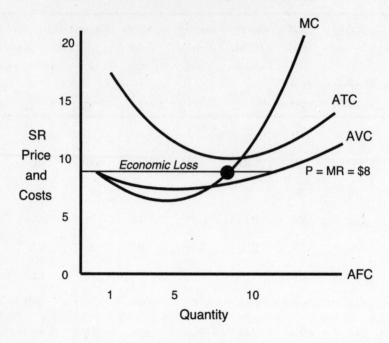

**Purely Competitive Firm:
Short-Run Economic Loss**

Figure 18

Individual firms believe that some firms will flee an industry because of loss, causing the industry supply curve to move up and inward. Because the industry has a downward sloping demand curve, prices would then rise, industry output would fall, and firms would return to normal profit (which occurs at a price of $8.60, due to the fact that at 7 units of output quantity, P = D = MR = MC at minimum ATC) in the long run. This can be seen in table 5 and figure 19, which depict the supply and demand of the industry as a whole, rather than for the individual firm.

Table 5

Total, Average, and Marginal Cost Schedules in Short Run

Total Output	Total Revenue	Total Costs	Average Fixed Costs	Average Variable Costs	Average Total Costs	Marginal Costs	Marginal Revenue = Price	Total Economic Profit+Loss
Q	TR = Price × Quantity	TC = TFC+TVC	$AFC=\dfrac{TFC}{Q}$	$AVC=\dfrac{TVC}{Q}$	$ATC=\dfrac{TC}{Q}$	$MC=\dfrac{\Delta TC}{\Delta Q}$	$MR=\dfrac{\Delta TR}{\Delta Q}$	TR–TC= Profit
0	0	$10						−10
1	8.60	20	$10	$10	$20	$10	$8.60	−11.40
2	17.20	28	5	9	14	8	8.60	−10.80
3	25.80	35	3.33	8.33	11.6	7	8.60	−32.20
4	34.40	40	2.5	7.5	10	5	8.60	−5.60
5	43.00	45	2	7	9	5	8.60	−2.00
6	51.60	51.96	1.66	7	8.66	7	8.60	−0.36
7	60.20	60.20	1.44	7.2	8.6	8.6	8.60	0
8	68.80	70.96	1.25	7.5	8.75	9.4	8.60	−2.16
9	77.40	90	1.1	8.8	10	20	8.60	−12.60

Purely Competitive Firm and Industry: Long-Run Normal Profit

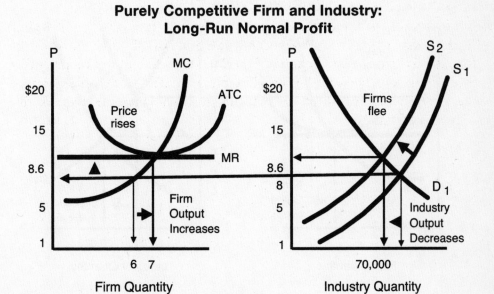

Figure 19

61

So too, if firms in a purely competitive market are experiencing economic profit, others will be attracted to the profit, moving the industry supply curve down and to the right. Again, because the industry has a downward sloping demand curve, prices will fall. This explains the long-run equilibrium concept of productive and allocative efficiency. Because firms are attracted to profit and repelled by loss, long-run equilibrium will occur at minimum ATC. Therefore, in the long-run, Price = D = MR = MC at minimum ATC and economic efficiency occurs (as shown in table 5 and figure 19). If firms are earning an economic profit, consumers are signaling the need for greater allocation of resources to this g/s. If firms are seeing losses, they should reduce their allocation of resources. If:

- P > MC, then resources are underallocated.

- P < MC, then resources are overallocated.

In the long run, society receives exactly what it wants, as the "invisible hands" work. The self-interest of producers and consumer satisfaction are maximized (productive efficiency and allocative efficiency).

What happens in the long run when the short-run price is $15? Supply increases and price returns to LR minimum ATC. Economic profit ends and normal profit returns to the industry.

Purely Competitive Firm and Industry:
Long-Run Normal Profit

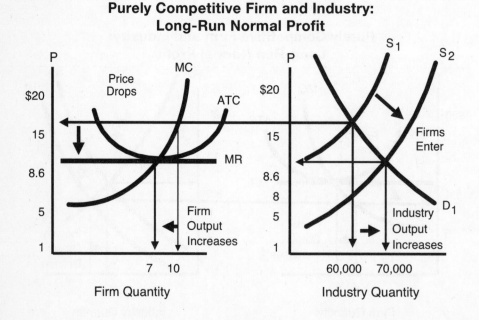

Figure 20

PURE MONOPOLY

A monopoly is an industry composed of a single firm selling a product for which there is no substitute. There are high barriers to entry into the industry, because the firm has resource control, or it may have government-granted patents and licenses. This firm has control over quantity and therefore can change price (price maker) by changing the quantity of product supplied, limited by the demand curve for the g/s. A natural monopoly occurs in industries where a declining long-run ATC curve extends over a high output quantity. This makes an individual producer more cost-efficient than several smaller firms, each producing lesser amounts. This is why economists refer to the monopolist as a "price maker." The monopolist seeks profit maximization, as all producers do. Its costs are the same, so it seeks the highest total profit, not the highest price. This is why the MR = MC rule still applies. The firm will charge the highest price possible for the level of output produced and demanded (see table 6).

Table 6

Short Run
Total and Marginal Cost, Total and Marginal Revenue Schedules

Total Output Q	Price Average Revenue Demand	Total Costs $TC = TFC+TVC$	Total Revenue $TR = Price \times Quantity$	Average Variable Costs $AVC = \dfrac{TVC}{Q}$	Average Total Costs $ATC = \dfrac{TC}{Q}$	Marginal Costs $MC = \dfrac{\Delta TC}{\Delta Q}$	Marginal Revenue = Price $MR = \dfrac{\Delta TR}{\Delta Q}$	Total Economic Profit+Loss $TR-TC=$ Profit
0	0	$10						−10
1	22	20	$ 22	$10	$20	$10	$22	2
2	20	28	40	9	14	8	18	12
3	18	35	54	8.33	11.6	7	14	19
4	16	40	64	7.5	10	5	10	24
5	14	45	70	7	9	5	6	25
6	12	52	72	7	8.66	7	2	20
7	10	60.6	70	7.2	8.6	8.6	−2	9.4
8	8	70	64	7.5	8.75	9.4	−6	−6
9	6	90	54	8.8	10	20	−10	−36

The monopolist will produce at the output quantity of 5 units, thus operating in the elastic total revenue portion of the demand curve. Remember that in the elastic portion, an increase in output increases the total revenue. The monopolist would not operate in the inelastic total revenue portion, as that price would result in a decrease in total revenue. As seen in table 6, any output quantity greater than 5 results in a decrease in total revenue because the consumer will not purchase that quantity (output of 6) unless the price is lowered ($12). The lower price results in a decrease in total revenue (inelastic) from $25 to $20, so the monopolist will not produce at that output level. This decision to limit production to 5 units results in maximum profitability for the firm. However, this is achieved through productive inefficiency (higher than minimum ATC) and allocative inefficiency (output below demand intersection with MC). These realities are confirmed in the model in figure 21. Note that MR = MC at a price above ATC. The shaded area represents the economic profit of the firm. If demand lessened, the monopolist could experience loss, if demand fell below ATC.

Pure Monopoly:
Long-Run Economic Profit

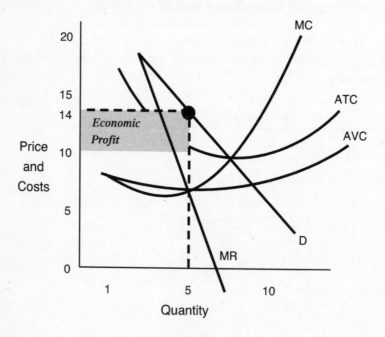

Figure 21

MONOPOLISTIC COMPETITION

Both the purely competitive and imperfectly competitive models are extremes. Most industries and producers fall between the two. Monopolistic competition exhibits considerable competition, but with some pricing power. Pricing power comes from a firm's product quality, recognition, location, and service; in other words, from product differentiation. Firms in differentiated competition are subject to the demand curve, and so output decisions greatly affect both price and profits. It is also important to note that the demand and marginal revenue curves are more elastic for the monopolistically competitive firm than for the monopoly. The monopolistic competitor maximizes profits or minimizes loss by producing at the output level where MR = MC. Long-run economic profit is difficult, as new firms will enter just as firms will flee loss. Thus, monopolistic competitors (similar to purely competitive) earn normal profits in the long run. Also, they achieve normal profit at slightly above minimum ATC (no productive efficiency) and with output at less than allocative efficiency (similar to pure monopoly). Their situation is depicted graphically in figure 22.

Monopolistic Competitive Firm and Industry: Long-Run Normal Profit

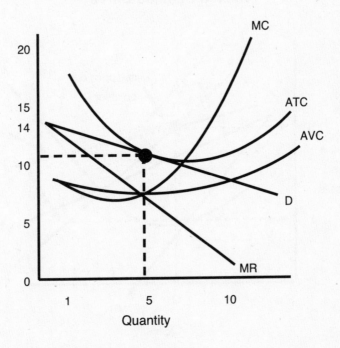

Figure 22

OLIGOPOLY

An *oligopoly* is an industry dominated by a few very large firms. These firms may have either homogenous products or differentiated ones. Regardless, they are bound by mutual dependence. They are interdependent because the profitability of each firm depends on the strategies pursued by its competitors. Each firm's pricing and output strategy is determined by the expected reaction of its business rivals. It is easy to understand why a firm attempting to maximize profits would attempt to collude with its competition. This collusion could be formal (planned) or informal (unplanned). Unplanned collusion is what prevents price wars from occurring. Price wars are explained best by the kinked demand curve (figure 23). The kinked demand curve illustrates how an oligopolist will refrain from raising its price left of the kink (where demand is relatively elastic). This would lower market share and total revenue for the oligopolist firm, as its competitors would not follow a price increase. However, if an oligopolist lowered its price right of the kink (where demand is relatively inelastic), it would not gain market share, because its competitors would tend to follow the price decrease.

Oligopoly:
Kinked Demand Curve

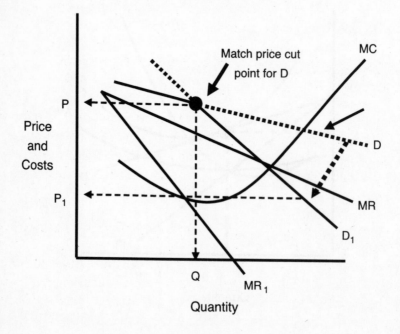

Figure 23

Noncollusive oligopolies believe that any price change is for the worse (raise price, lose customers/lower price, lose revenue), so they seek stable prices. Often a firm that begins incurring higher costs will attempt or announce an intended price hike ("price leader") and then respond to its rivals' behavior. In some situations, when a rival is in a weakened condition (carrying a high debt load, for example), a firm may engage in a price war to force the rival out of business or into a merger.

CARTELS

It is easy to understand why firms would be willing to act together to avoid price wars. When acting as one, they in essence are a monopoly. Price can be dictated through output limits. This behavior is illegal in the United States and therefore would have to be undertaken secretly to fix prices. OPEC is the best example of an ongoing cartel; this group of 11 major oil producers, led by Saudi Arabia, attempts to control oil prices through overt agreement on each producer's output quota. At times, such as in 1974, 1978, and in mid-2000, output cutbacks by OPEC caused prices to rise sharply. These higher oil prices have been difficult for OPEC to maintain in the long run, however. There are obstacles to the success of cartels, such as members having different production efficiencies, higher prices attracting new firms, substitutes being developed, conflict between members, members secretly cheating, or the consumer's economy slumping into recession because of the higher costs being forced upon it.

PRICING AND EMPLOYMENT OF FACTOR MARKETS

Remember the importance of the factor (resource) market in the circular flow of g/s in a free market economy. Firms purchase their input factors (land, labor, capital, and entrepreneurial management) from households. To predict the pricing of inputs, we have to examine the nature of the demand and supply for those inputs.

MARGINAL RESOURCE PRODUCTIVITY THEORY

Marginal resource productivity theory is built upon the premise that supply of and demand for inputs is purely competitive. To a producer, the demand for resource inputs is a derived demand. The value of the resource input is determined by the demand for the g/s that the input is used to produce. Therefore, the demand for an input will depend on:

- The productivity of the input in creating the finished g/s.

- The price of the finished g/s that has been produced by the resource input.

For the sake of simplicity, let's use the resource input of labor for this review. A producer would record the increasing units of labor and the resultant change in total output. This allows us to calculate the marginal product. Assuming that the market price of the finished good remains constant, we can also calculate the total revenue at each level of output and thus the marginal revenue product (MRP). The formula is:

$$MRP = \frac{\text{change in TR}}{\text{unit change in resource quantity}}$$

If we also calculate the amount that each additional unit of labor input adds to the producer's total cost, we get its marginal resource cost (MRC). The formula is:

$$MRC = \frac{\text{change in total input cost}}{\text{unit change in input quantity}}$$

A firm would use the profit-maximizing strategy of hiring one more worker, as long as the worker's contribution to revenue exceeded the increased cost to the firm (MRP = MRC). This can be viewed in table 7.

Table 7

Units of Resource Labor Inputs	Total Product Output	Marginal Product	Product Price	Total Revenue	Marginal Revenue Product	Marginal Resource Cost *assume each employee receives same wage of $125*
1	6	6	$100	$600	$600	$125
2	19	13	100	1,900	1,300	125
3	25	6	100	2,500	600	125
4	29	4	100	2,900	400	125
5	31	2	100	3,100	200	125
6	32	1	100	3,200	100	125
7	32	0	100	3,200	0	125

This firm would hire 5 units of resource labor inputs, because the fifth employee contributes more revenue ($200) than he adds in cost ($125). If a sixth employee were added, her contribution to revenue ($100) would be less than her added cost ($125), thereby decreasing the firm's profit.

Our analyses of a producer's behavior become more complicated in the real world, as neither product prices nor resource costs are purely competitive. As shown in table 8, not only do product prices decrease as more units are sold, but labor prices also increase as more workers are hired. Nonetheless, the firm would still operate at the profit-maximizing level where MRP ≥ MRC. In this case, 4 units of labor would be employed.

Table 8

Units of Resource Labor Inputs	Total Product Output	Marginal Product	Product Price	Total Revenue	Marginal Revenue Product	Total Labor Cost *assume with each added employee wage costs increase by $10*	Marginal Resource Cost
1	6	6	$280	$1680	$1,680	(60) 60	$60
2	19	13	260	4,940	3,260	(70) 140	80
3	25	6	240	6,000	1,060	(80) 240	100
4	29	4	220	6,380	380	(90) 360	120
5	31	2	200	6,200	−180	(100) 500	140
6	32	1	185	5,920	−280	(110) 660	160
7	32	0	185	5,920	0	(120) 840	180

At this point, we need to consider the reality that resources are combined in production. For example, how do firms balance the inputs of capital with labor inputs to minimize costs? Firms will seek a least-cost combination of resources that will produce an equal marginal product with the last dollar expended on each resource. In other words:

$$\frac{\text{Marginal Product of Labor (MP}_L)}{\text{Price of Labor (P}_L)} = \frac{\text{Marginal Product of Capital (MP}_C)}{\text{Price of Capital (P}_C)}$$

If the MP_L was 6 and the MP_C was 3, and each had a price of $1, what should a firm do?

Since $\dfrac{6}{1} > \dfrac{3}{1}$, the firm should spend less on capital and more on labor.

If it spent nothing on capital, the firm would lose 3 units. It would recapture those lost units by spending $0.50 more on labor, yielding a cost savings of $0.50 to the firm.

To determine the profit-maximizing combination of two factors of production, a firm must employ each resource (factor) to the point that its marginal revenue product equals its price. Using the formula,

$$\frac{MRP_L}{P_L} = \frac{MRP_C}{P_C} = 1,$$

the profit-maximizing blend could be achieved. Note that when applying the profit-maximizing equation, a firm is also employing the least-cost combination. However, the reverse is not necessarily the case. A firm operating at least-cost with multiple factors may not be operating at profit-maximizing output levels. Again, a table can be used to demonstrate the formula at work (table 9).

Table 9

Units of Resource Labor Inputs	Total Product Output	Marginal Product	Total Revenue ($2)	MRP_L Price of $4	Total Product Output	Marginal Product	Total Revenue ($2)	Marginal Price of $12
1	6	6	13	13	13	13	$26	$26
2	19	13	38	25	22	9	44	18
3	25	6	50	22	28	6	56	12
4	29	4	58	8	32	4	64	8
5	31	2	62	4	35	3	70	6
6	32	1	64	2	37	2	74	4
7	32	0	64	0	38	1	76	2

Least-cost profit maximizing would occur for the firm when it combines 5 units of labor with 3 units of capital. In algebraic form,

$$\frac{MRP_L \, 4}{\$4} = \frac{MRP_C \, 12}{\$12} = 1.$$

Let's compare this X combination of 5 units of labor (producing 31 units with revenue of \$62) and (5 × \$4 =) \$20 cost with 3 capital (producing 28 units with revenue of \$56) and (3 × \$12 =) \$36 cost to another combination, Y. The X blend has a TR of \$118 minus a TC of \$56 and a profit of \$62.

The Y combination of 3 units of labor (producing 25 units with revenue of \$50) and (3 × \$4 =) \$12 cost with 3 capital (producing 28 units with revenue of \$56) and (3 × \$12 =) \$36 cost. The Y combination has a TR of \$106 minus a TC of \$48 and a lesser profit of \$58. The X combination is the least-cost, maximum-profit combination of resource inputs.

THE LABOR MARKET AND WAGES

Most Americans are concerned about the labor market in general, particularly labor supply and wage and employment determination. Your wage determines your standard of living. The first important distinction regarding income is the difference between nominal (dollar amount of wage) and real wages (quantity of g/s your wage purchases). With this in mind, it is easy to see the direct relationship between increased productivity, real wages, and rising standards of living. By applying the previous concepts of determination of factor prices (derived demand), an economist explains the sources of income inequality in a market economy. Some workers compete in perfectly competitive labor markets. Others experience the effect of deviations from perfect competition, such as minimum wage laws, the union effect, and monopsony.

PURELY COMPETITIVE LABOR MARKET

In a purely competitive market, the laws of supply and demand are at work (remember that the demand for labor is the MRP of labor), and they determine the wage rate and quantity of workers hired in an industry. The industry wage rate would be determined by supply and demand would be perfectly elastic to the individual firm and therefore determine its MRC. So, for example, if the industry demand (MRP) for labor increased, the wage paid and the number of workers hired within an industry would also increase (figure 24).

Purely Competitive Firm and Industry
Labor Costs—Hourly $ Wage Rate

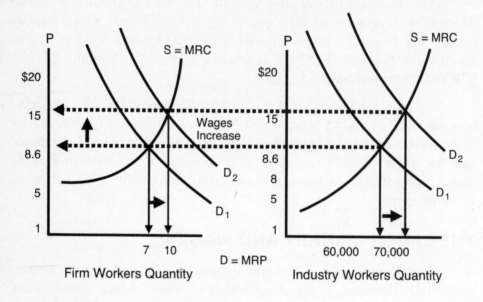

Figure 24

MONOPSONY

Monopsony is a market situation in which there is just one buyer of a resource input. A monopsonistic firm hires an additional unit of labor as long as its MRC = MRP. A monopsonist has an upward sloping supply curve of labor. This means that to hire an additional unit of labor, it must pay that worker a higher wage. When the monopsonist pays the new worker the higher wage, it must also pay that wage to all the workers it currently employs (because current workers would be extremely dissatisfied if a new worker outearned them). This means that the MRC of the new worker is equal to the new worker's wage added to the amount necessary to bring all current workers to that new wage as well. This is important because now the MRC curve lies above the supply of workers, unlike the purely competitive market where supply equaled MRC. Therefore, the least-cost, profit-maximizing formula previously stated will apply: namely, MRC = MRP = 1. The monopsonist maximizes profits by both hiring and paying labor at its MRC = MRP wage rate and quantity, not the supply equilibrium rate or quantity. In other words, the monopsonist underhires and underpays market price and quantity of labor. Figure 25 demonstrates this concept.

Monopsonist Labor Market

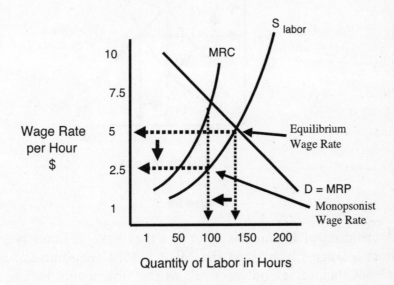

Figure 25

Notice that the monopsonist hires the quantity of resource labor, 100 workers, and pays the lower rate of $2.50 (MRP = MRC), rather than the 150 workers at $5.00-per-hour wage equilibrium for a purely competitive market firm. The monopsonistic firm is looking to maximize profits by paying labor less than its MRP.

UNION EFFECT

Unions affect the labor market in several ways, but perhaps the foremost is by limiting the supply of labor that a firm can draw upon. This restriction of labor supply (S to S_1) can extract a higher wage at the MRP = MRC equilibrium. This higher wage comes at the price of jobs, in that the higher cost causes a firm to hire fewer workers than it would in a nonunion market. Figure 26 illustrates this situation.

Unionized Labor Market

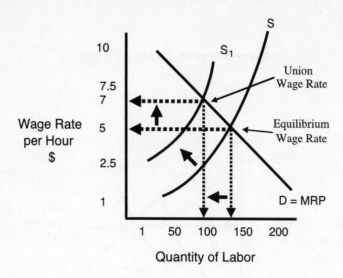

Figure 26

A criticism of unions has been that they have at times been able to extract a wage higher than the MRP = MRC equilibrium, and in essence put themselves out of work as the firm incurs loss or faces nonunion competition. Without question, union membership (13.5%) has declined as a percentage of the workforce. Many unions argue that this is the result of firms taking work overseas to less industrialized, lower-wage, nonunionized nations. Nevertheless, many workers still collectively bargain their wages and benefits. All workers are protected by federal labor law and the National Labor Relations Board (NLRB) investigates reports of abuse of workers.

MINIMUM WAGE LAWS

Government intervention into the purely competitive market for labor would act much the same as our earlier model of rent controls. If minimum wage were set above equilibrium ($10), firms would hire fewer workers (25) and the workers seeking those jobs (125) would be numerous. Conversely, if minimum wage were below equilibrium, firms would seek to pay down to the legal wage, but few workers would be interested in working at that price. This can be viewed graphically in figure 27.

Minimum Wage Law Above Market Equilibrium

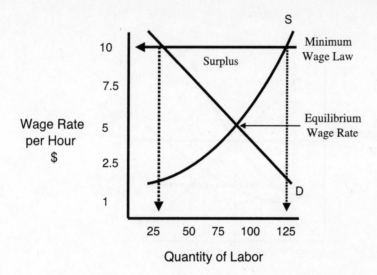

Figure 27

In the minimum wage scenario, the demand for labor at $10 per hour would be very low, whereas the number of job seekers would be extremely high. This minimum wage would result in a surplus of labor. This is one of the main arguments against minimum wage.

Proponents counter this argument by pointing out that, in the real world, the affected low-pay labor market is subject to some monopsony power. As shown in figure 28, the monopsonist firm would hire 150 hours of labor and pay workers $5 per hour (MRC), even though they generate $10 in revenue (MRP), and thus create economic profit. The wage could be increased to $10 without causing unemployment, as the firm could afford to pay $10 and still make a normal profit.

Minimum Wage Law (Some Monopsony)

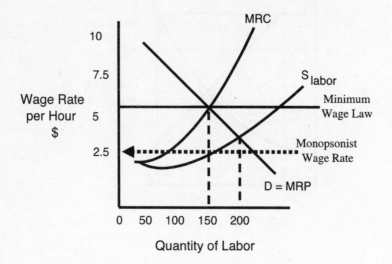

Figure 28

INCOME INEQUALITY AND POVERTY

Advocates of government wage intervention suggest that the income disparity resulting from the free market is too great. The debate over how much disparity between rich and poor should be allowed to exist is ongoing (refer to fiscal policy review). Furthermore, there is additional heated argument over what method to use to address this inequity issue, and to what extent. The most widely used measure to demonstrate income distribution over time is the Lorenz curve, shown in figure 29. The Lorenz curve contrasts five equal percentile groupings of population with their percentage share of total income. The income used is before tax and includes cash transfer payments; it does not include noncash transfers (food stamps, Medicaid, etc.). A bisection of the graph provides a perfectly direct relationship between population and income of that population. Therefore, the greater the actual distribution curve bows outward from the diagonal line, the greater the degree of income inequality.

The Lorenz Curve

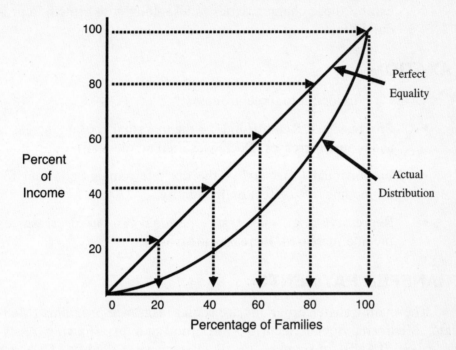

Figure 29

U.S. income distribution is significantly more equal than the Lorenz curve for the world as a whole. Proponents of increased government intervention for more even distribution of income advocate increased progressive income taxes, transfer payments, aid to education, and laws designed to end discrimination. Critics of this analysis believe that several flaws are present in this contention, including:

- Arbitrary income limits for income categories.

- Time frame fails to account for changes in earnings over lifetime.

- Income is nominal and does not account for an overall rise in the standard of living. (It measures your percentage piece of the pie, not the overall size of the pie, which might have increased.)

- Income does not measure changes in other assets that constitute wealth.

- Higher incomes reflect behaviors that result in high productivity. Remove the resulting income, and the incentive to exhibit those characteristics fades, along with growth in productivity.

TAXATION

Taxes are divided into three groups:

- Progressive ("Robin Hood")—the marginal tax rate increases as income increases. Decreases income inequality.

- Proportional ("flat tax")—the tax rate remains constant for all incomes. No effect on inequality.

- Regressive (e.g., sales tax)—marginal tax rate decreases as income increases. Increases inequality.

TRANSFER PAYMENTS

The main transfer programs are social insurance programs (Medicaid, Medicare, Social Security, SSI, food stamps, Housing Assistance, and TANF) guaranteed to all citizens who qualify. They are entitled to the benefits of these programs by law. Many people qualify because of a disability, illness, unemployment, or other specified misfortune. Other people receive aid from welfare programs, the largest of which is Temporary Assistance for Needy Families (TANF), which recently replaced Aid to Families with Dependent Children (AFDC). The cost of these programs has been increasing at a rapid rate. The funding of these programs continues to be a major source of discussion between political parties. The effectiveness of these programs in reducing poverty depends on the measurement criteria. Some argue that without assistance, human suffering would be much greater. Others point out that public assistance is a disincentive to work and improve one's economic condition, which leads to dependency on the welfare system.

ANTIDISCRIMINATION LAWS

Disparate income for women and minorities is a matter of historical record. The government has several means by which it can encourage equal employment opportunity to end discrimination: maintain full employment, improve educational or training opportunities, and mandate practices that assist statistical equality. Beginning in 1963 with the Equal Pay Act, and continuing with Title VII of the 1964 Civil

Rights Act, and affirmative action required by Executive Orders of 1965 and 1968, proponents believe much good has been done in addressing unequal opportunity in America. Some argue that more should be done in the future. Opponents, of affirmative action in particular, point out that this preferential treatment is reverse discrimination. A series of federal and Supreme Court cases upheld the constitutionality of affirmative action in 1986 and 1987, but reignited the debate in 1995 when the Supreme Court ruled that public universities may not justify quotas based on the benefits of diversity. Some states, such as California and Washington, have amended their laws to end gender or racial preferences.

GOVERNMENT INTERVENTION

In addition to the intervention already reviewed, other shortcomings in the free market system may be addressed by further government action. These shortcomings are dealt with through public goods, production standards, and regulation of business practices.

PUBLIC GOODS

Certain goods and services are difficult or impossible to deliver through the free market, as there is no profit incentive for private production thereof. Adam Smith recognized this, and mentioned defense, roads, education, and medical care as being among them. Public goods are neither divisible nor exclusionary (there is shared consumption and nonexclusion). It would be difficult to charge on an individual basis for law enforcement, courts, airports, or fighter planes. Therefore, goods that provide for the common good fall into this category. Disagreement over the nature and extent of these g/s is present today. Some argue that public goods such as education are not best delivered by government, but rather should be held to federal standards and privatized through a voucher system.

NEGATIVE AND POSITIVE EXTERNALITIES

Economists describe (spillover) costs or (spillover) benefits that are borne by parties not directly associated with an economic activity in the marketplace as *externalities*. An example of a spillover benefit is public flu shots. Even though you may not receive a shot, your exposure is diminished as a result, and you will not have to help pay the hospital costs for those who would have gotten sick. A spillover cost is the pollution that results from production of a good that spews sulfur into the air. There is no direct cost. Government can tax the polluter to cover the cost of clean air, or even require prevention of the pollution in the first place, through environmental standards. Many government taxes and subsidies are employed to encourage or discourage economic activities with externalities.

GOVERNMENT INDUSTRIAL REGULATION

Government at the end of the nineteenth century concluded that some individuals had created companies that monopolized market forces in a way that was detrimental to society. Therefore, a series of antitrust laws (Sherman, 1890; Clayton, 1914; Federal Trade Commission Act, 1914; and the Celler-Kefauver Act, 1950) were passed that together provide the legal basis for government regulation of business. The FTC and the Justice Department each help protect the degree of competition necessary for the free market to operate efficiently. We have already reviewed the natural tendency of firms to seek merger in order to maximize profits. Government can act to prevent mergers or to break up firms that violate acceptable levels of competition. In the 1980s, much relaxation of enforcement resulted in deregulation of some firms (airlines, utilities) and allowed increased concentration in others (food and beverage).

MERGER TYPES

There are three basic types of merger: horizontal, merging two similar producers; vertical, merging two firms that are part of a goods production process; and conglomerate, merging different industries or multinational companies. Firms seeking mergers of this latter nature must seek government approval prior to conclusion of any agreement. If denied, they may appeal through the court system. This has become increasingly complicated, as the United States may approve a merger only to have it denied by the European Union (as with the proposed GE and Honeywell merger), and vice versa.

▼

MICROECONOMICS
TEST

AP Microeconomics

Test

Section I

TIME: 70 minutes
         60 multiple-choice questions

(Answer sheets appear in the back of this book.)

DIRECTIONS: Each of the questions or incomplete statements below is followed by five suggested answers or completions. Select the best answer for each question and then fill in the corresponding oval on the answer sheet.

---

1.   The primary focus of microeconomics is

  (A)   the aggregate supply and aggregate demand resultant output.

  (B)   unlimited resources and unlimited wants.

  (C)   the specific economic components that make up the economic system.

  (D)   concealment of detailed information about specific segments of the economy.

  (E)   manipulating overall performance of the economic system.

2.   Economic efficiency is mainly concerned with

  (A)   the limited wants–unlimited resources dilemma.

  (B)   considerations of equity in the distribution of wealth.

  (C)   obtaining the maximum output from available resources.

      (D)   creating the greatest societal satisfaction from resources.

      (E)   the transfer of wealth in an equitable fashion.

3.   A production possibilities curve is "bowed out" from the origin because

      (A)   input resources are not equally efficient in producing two alternative goods.

      (B)   Keynes recognized this reality and modern economists follow his theory.

      (C)   specialization of output increases input potential.

      (D)   resources are scarce.

      (E)   wants are virtually unlimited.

4.   Opportunity cost

      (A)   is reflected in the convex curve of cost models.

      (B)   does not apply to socialistic economies, because of central planning.

      (C)   suggests that the use of resources in any particular line of production means that alternative outputs must be forgone.

      (D)   is irrelevant if the production possibilities curve is shifting to the right.

      (E)   suggests that insatiable wants can be fulfilled.

Circular Flow Model

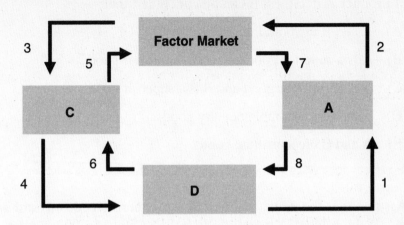

5. In the preceding circular flow model of a free market economy, flow (4) represents

    (A) wage, rent, interest, and profit income.

    (B) land, labor, capital, and entrepreneurial ability.

    (C) goods and services brought to the product market.

    (D) consumer expenditures.

    (E) costs of production.

6. "As the retail price of a good increases, consumers shift their purchases to other products whose prices are now relatively lower." This statement describes

    (A) an inferior good.

    (B) the rationing function of prices.

    (C) the substitution effect.

    (D) opportunity cost.

    (E) the income effect.

7. If the demand curve for product B shifts to the right as the price of product A declines, it can be concluded that

   (A) A and B are both inferior goods.

   (B) A is a superior good and B is an inferior good.

   (C) A is an inferior good and B is a superior good.

   (D) A and B are complementary goods.

   (E) A and B are substitute goods.

8. Assume that the demand schedule for concrete is downward sloping. If the price of concrete falls from $2.50 to $2.00 a pound

   (A) the quantity demanded of concrete will decrease.

   (B) the demand for concrete will decrease.

   (C) the quantity demanded of concrete will increase.

   (D) the demand for concrete will increase.

   (E) the demand for concrete will shift to the left.

9. Assume that a drought in Kansas reduces the supply of barley. Barley is a basic ingredient in the production of beer, and wine is a consumer substitute for beer. Therefore, we would expect the price of beer to

   (A) rise, the supply of beer to increase, and the demand for wine to increase.

   (B) rise, the supply of beer to decrease, and the demand for wine to increase.

   (C) rise, the supply of beer to decrease, and the demand for wine to decrease.

   (D) fall, the supply of beer to increase, and the demand for wine to increase.

   (E) None of the above.

Vanilla Ice Cream Market

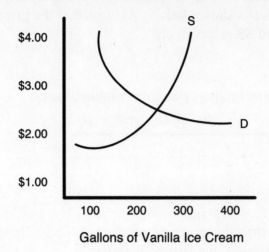

Gallons of Vanilla Ice Cream

10. Refer to the preceding diagram. The equilibrium price and quantity in the vanilla ice cream market will be approximately

   (A) $1.00 and 200.

   (B) $1.60 and 130.

   (C) $0.50 and 130.

   (D) $1.60 and 290.

   (E) $2.50 and 250.

11. Specialization in production is desirable because it

   (A) allows everyone to have a job that he or she likes.

   (B) permits the production of a larger output with fixed amounts of resources.

   (C) facilitates trade by bartering.

   (D) increases output of goods at higher prices.

   (E) guarantees full employment.

Answer question 12 on the basis of the following information: Suppose 30 units of product A can be produced by employing just labor and capital in the 4 ways shown below. Assume that the prices of labor and capital are $2 and $3 respectively.

Production techniques possible combinations:

	I	II	III	IV
Labor	4	3	2	5
Capital	2	3	5	1

12. Assuming that the price of product A is $0.50 and that all 30 units will be sold, the firm will realize

    (A) an economic profit of $4.

    (B) an economic profit of $2.

    (C) an economic profit of $6.

    (D) a loss of $6.

    (E) a loss of $3.

13. Assume that a normal good is being produced in a competitive industry that is in long-run equilibrium. If average consumer income increased, which of the following combinations would result?

	Output	Price	# of firms in industry
(A)	Decrease	Decrease	Exit
(B)	Decrease	Decrease	Enter
(C)	Increase	Decrease	Exit
(D)	Decrease	Increase	Exit
(E)	Increase	Increase	Enter

14. The free market system does not produce public goods because

   I.   There is inadequate demand for such goods.

   II.   People who do not pay for the goods cannot be prevented from consuming them.

   III. Collecting revenue from production of such goods is difficult.

   (A) I only.

   (B) II only.

   (C) III only.

   (D) Both I and III.

   (E) Both II and III.

15. The price of product X is reduced from $100 to $90. As a result, the quantity demanded increases from 50 to 60 units. Therefore, demand for X in this price elasticity range

   (A) has declined.

   (B) is of unit elasticity.

   (C) is inelastic.

   (D) results in lower total revenue for firms.

   (E) is elastic.

16. Suppose that a 20 percent increase in the price of normal good Y causes a 10 percent decline in the quantity demanded of normal good X. The coefficient of cross elasticity of demand is

   (A) negative, and therefore these goods are substitutes.

   (B) negative, and thus income sensitive.

   (C) negative, and therefore these goods are complements.

   (D) positive, and therefore these goods are substitutes.

   (E) positive, and therefore these goods are complements.

17. Assume that a 3 percent increase in income in the economy produces a 1 percent decline in the quantity demanded of good X. The outcome would be

Coefficient of Income Elasticity	Type of Good X is:
(A) negative	inferior good
(B) negative	normal good
(C) positive	inferior good
(D) positive	normal good
(E) negative	unrelated

18. The first sport drink yields Craig 18 units of utility and the second yields him an additional 12 units of utility. His total utility from three sport drinks is 36 units of utility. The marginal utility of the third sport drink is

(A) 26 units of utility.

(B) 6 units of utility.

(C) 8 units of utility.

(D) 54 total utils.

(E) 38 total utils.

Answer questions 19 and 20 on the basis of the following table, which shows the amounts of additional satisfaction (marginal utility) that a consumer derives from successive quantities of products X and Y.

Units of X	MU_X	Units of Y	MU_Y
1	56	1	32
2	48	2	28
3	32	3	24
4	24	4	20
5	20	5	12
6	16	6	10
7	12	7	8

19. Refer to the preceding data. If the consumer has a money income of $52 and the prices of X and Y are $8 and $4 respectively, the consumer will maximize her utility by purchasing

    (A) 2 units of X and 7 units of Y.

    (B) 5 units of X and 5 units of Y.

    (C) 4 units of X and 5 units of Y.

    (D) 3 units of X and 6 units of Y.

    (E) 6 units of X and 3 units of Y.

20. Suppose that MU_X/P_X is greater than MU_Y/P_Y. To maximize utility, consumers who are spending their entire budget should alter their consumption so that they purchase

    (A) less of X, but only if its price rises.

    (B) more of Y, but only if its price rises.

    (C) more of Y and less of X.

    (D) neither; it should utilize the savings utility.

    (E) more of X and less of Y.

21. "Total cost," for an economist, includes

    (A) explicit and implicit costs, including a normal profit.

    (B) neither implicit nor explicit costs.

    (C) implicit, but not explicit, costs.

    (D) explicit, but not implicit, costs.

    (E) explicit and implicit costs, including an economic profit.

22. The main characteristic of supply in the short run is that

    (A) barriers to entry prevent new firms from entering the industry.

    (B) the firm does not have sufficient time to change the size of its plant.

(C) the firm does not have sufficient time to cut its rate of output to zero.

(D) a firm does not have sufficient time to change the amounts of any of the resources it employs.

(E) revenue is fixed.

23. Marginal product is

(A) the increase in total output attributable to the employment of one more worker.

(B) the increase in total revenue attributable to the employment of one more worker.

(C) the increase in total product divided by the change in revenue.

(D) the increase in total cost attributable to the employment of one more worker.

(E) total product divided by the number of workers employed.

24. The law of diminishing returns indicates that

(A) as revenue increases with each sale, total revenue declines.

(B) as extra units of a variable resource are added to a fixed resource, marginal product will decline beyond some point.

(C) because of economies and diseconomies of scale, a competitive firm's long-run average total cost curve will be U-shaped.

(D) the demand for goods produced by purely competitive industries is downsloping.

(E) beyond some point, the extra utility derived from additional units of a product will yield the consumer smaller and smaller extra amounts of satisfaction.

Answer question 25 on the basis of the following output data for a firm. Assume that the amounts of all nonlabor resources are fixed.

Number of Workers	Units of Output
0	0
1	40
2	90
3	126
4	150
5	165
6	180

25. Refer to the preceding data. The marginal product of the sixth worker is

    (A)   180 units of output.

    (B)   30 units of output.

    (C)   45 units of output.

    (D)   15 units of output.

    (E)   negative 15 units of output.

26. Marginal product

    (A)   diminishes at all levels of production.

    (B)   increases at all levels of production.

    (C)   may initially increase, then diminish, but never become negative.

    (D)   may initially increase, then diminish, and ultimately become negative.

    (E)   is always less than average product.

27. If you owned a small farm, which of the following would be a fixed cost?

    (A) Farm workers

    (B) Flood insurance

    (C) Gasoline

    (D) Pesticide

    (E) Seed

28. If you operated a small pizzeria, which of the following would be a variable cost in the short run?

    (A) Baking ovens

    (B) Interest on business loans

    (C) Annual lease payment for use of the building

    (D) Cheese toppings

    (E) Fire insurance

29. Marginal cost is the

    (A) rate of change in total fixed cost that results from producing one more unit of output.

    (B) change in total cost that results from producing one more unit of output.

    (C) increase in revenue caused by one more unit being consumed.

    (D) change in average variable cost that results from producing one more unit of output.

    (E) change in average total cost that results from producing one more unit of output.

30. Average fixed cost

    (A) equals marginal cost when average total cost is at its minimum.

    (B) may be found for any output by adding average variable cost and average total cost.

    (C) at some point begins to increase as output reduces.

    (D) is graphed as a U-shaped curve.

    (E) declines continually as output increases.

Individual Firm—Purely Competitive Market

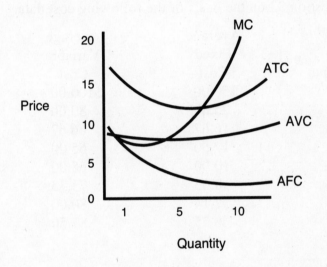

31. Refer to the preceding diagram. The vertical distance between ATC and AVC reflects

    (A) the law of diminishing returns.

    (B) the break-even point.

    (C) the average fixed cost at each level of output.

    (D) marginal cost at each level of output.

    (E) the presence of economies of scale.

32. If a technological advance reduces the amount of labor needed to produce an increased level of output, then

(A) the AVC curve will shift upward.

(B) the MC curve will shift upward.

(C) the ATC curve will shift downward.

(D) the AFC curve will shift upward.

(E) all of the above will occur.

Answer question 33 on the basis of the following cost data.

Output	Average Fixed Cost	Average Variable Cost
1	$50.00	$100.00
2	25.00	80.00
3	16.67	66.67
4	12.50	65.00
5	10.00	68.00
6	8.33	73.33
7	7.14	80.00
8	6.25	87.50

33. Based upon the preceding table, if the firm decided to increase its output from 6 to 7 units, by how much would its total costs rise?

(A) $170.00

(B) $80.00

(C) $6.67

(D) $120.02

(E) $108.02

34. In the short run, a purely competitive firm that seeks to maximize profit will produce

    (A) where marginal revenue intersects demand.

    (B) where the demand and ATC curves intersect.

    (C) where total revenue exceeds total cost by the maximum amount.

    (D) that output where economic profits are zero.

    (E) at any point where the total revenue and total cost curves intersect.

35. A firm reaches a breakeven point (normal profit position) where

    (A) marginal revenue cuts the horizontal axis.

    (B) marginal cost intersects the average variable cost curve.

    (C) total revenue equals total variable cost.

    (D) total revenue and total cost are equal.

    (E) total revenue equals all explicit costs.

36. The MR = MC rule applies

    (A) to firms in all types of industries.

    (B) to firms only in a natural monopoly.

    (C) only when the firm is a "price taker."

    (D) only to monopolies.

    (E) only to purely competitive firms.

Answer question 37 on the basis of the following data confronting a firm.

Output	Marginal Revenue	Marginal Cost
0	—	—
1	$16	$10
2	16	9
3	16	13
4	16	17
5	16	21

37. Refer to the preceding data. If the firm's minimum average variable cost is $10, the firm's profit-maximizing level of output would be

(A) 2.

(B) 3.

(C) 4.

(D) 5.

(E) 1.

Firm's Costs

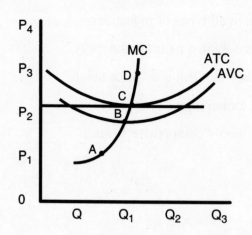

38. Refer to the preceding diagram for a purely competitive producer. The lowest price at which the firm should produce (as opposed to shutting down)

    (A) is P_1.

    (B) is P_2.

    (C) is P_3.

    (D) is P_4.

    (E) is P_5.

Answer question 39 on the basis of the following cost data for a firm that is selling in a purely competitive market.

Total Product	Average Fixed Cost	Average Variable Cost	Total Cost	Marginal Cost
1	$100.00	$17.00	$117.00	$17
2	50.00	16.00	66.00	15
3	33.33	15.00	48.33	13
4	25.00	14.25	39.25	12
5	20.00	14.00	34.00	13
6	16.67	14.00	30.67	14
7	14.29	15.71	30.00	26
8	12.50	17.50	30.00	30
9	11.11	19.44	30.55	35
10	10.00	21.60	31.60	41
11	9.09	24.00	33.09	48
12	8.33	26.67	35.00	56

39. Refer to the preceding data. If the market price for the firm's product is $42, the purely competitive firm will

    (A) produce 8 units at an economic profit of $16.

    (B) produce 5 units at a loss of $10.40.

    (C) produce 10 units at an economic profit of $104.

    (D) produce 8 units at a loss equal to the firm's total fixed cost.

    (E) produce 7 units at an economic profit of $41.50.

40. The short-run shutdown point for a purely competitive firm occurs

    (A) at any point where price is less than the minimum AVC.

    (B) between the two breakeven points.

    (C) at any point where total revenue is greater than total cost.

    (D) at any point below normal profit.

    (E) at any point where the firm is not making an economic profit.

Answer question 41 on the basis of the following cost data for a purely competitive seller.

Total Product	Total Fixed Cost	Total Variable Cost	Total Cost
0	$50	$0	$50
1	50	70	120
2	50	120	170
3	50	150	200
4	50	220	270
5	50	300	350
6	50	390	440

41. Refer to the preceding data. What is the marginal cost of the fifth unit of output?

    (A) $80

    (B) $90

    (C) $50

    (D) $70

    (E) $20

42. We would expect an industry to expand if firms in that industry are

    (A) meeting explicit and implicit costs.

    (B) earning normal profits.

    (C) earning economic profits.

    (D) realizing an equality of total revenue and total costs.

    (E) earning accounting profits.

43. A firm is producing at an output where the revenue gain from the last unit produced is less than the cost of producing that additional unit. This firm is

    (A) producing more output than allocative efficiency requires.

    (B) producing at an output that does not cover explicit costs.

    (C) producing less output than allocative efficiency requires.

    (D) realizing productive efficiency.

    (E) producing an inefficient output, but we cannot say whether output should be increased or decreased.

Firm's Costs

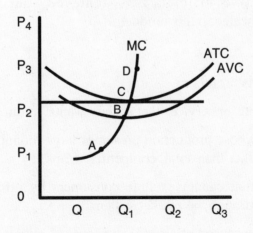

44. Refer to the preceding diagram. By producing at output level Q_1 in a purely competitive environment

    (A) the firm is operating below shut-down level.

    (B) neither productive nor allocative efficiency is achieved.

    (C) both productive and allocative efficiency are achieved.

    (D) allocative efficiency is achieved, but productive efficiency is not.

    (E) productive efficiency is achieved, but allocative efficiency is not.

45. Refer to the preceding diagram. At output level Q_2 in a purely competitive environment

    (A) the firm is operating below shut-down level.

    (B) resources are overallocated to this product and productive efficiency is not realized.

    (C) resources are underallocated to this product and productive efficiency is not realized.

    (D) productive efficiency is achieved, but resources are underallocated to this product.

    (E) productive efficiency is achieved, but resources are overallocated to this product.

46. "Public goods" refers to

    (A) any goods or services that society wants produced.

    (B) goods whose production presumes large monopolistic corporations rather than small competitive firms.

    (C) goods that cannot exclude consumers by price and are produced through the market system.

    (D) goods produced at an efficient level of output due to elimination of competition.

    (E) goods that are produced using minimal amounts of society's scarce resources.

Market Model

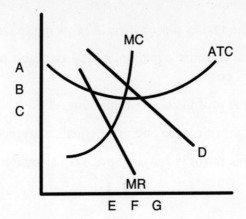

47. Refer to the preceding diagram. To maximize profits or minimize losses, this firm should produce

    (A) E units and charge price C.

    (B) E units and charge price A.

    (C) F units and charge price B.

    (D) G units and charge price C.

    (E) E units and charge price B.

48. An important economic problem associated with pure monopoly is that, at profit-maximizing outputs, resources are

    (A) overallocated, because price exceeds marginal cost.

    (B) overallocated, because price is less than demand.

    (C) overallocated, because marginal cost exceeds price.

    (D) underallocated, because price exceeds marginal cost.

    (E) underallocated, because marginal cost exceeds price.

49. When a monopolistically competitive firm is in long-run equilibrium

    (A) production takes place where ATC is minimized.

    (B) marginal revenue equals marginal cost and price equals average total cost.

    (C) economic profit is above minimum ATC.

    (D) normal profit is zero and price equals marginal cost.

    (E) economic profit is zero and price equals marginal cost.

50. In the long run, new firms will enter a monopolistically competitive industry

    (A) provided economies of scale are being realized.

    (B) even though losses are incurred in the short run.

    (C) until minimum average total cost is achieved.

    (D) as long as minimum AVC is met and shut-down is avoided.

    (E) until economic profits are zero.

51. Cartels are difficult to maintain in the long run because

    (A) they are illegal in all industrialized countries.

    (B) firms realize that profits would increase if they secretly increase output.

    (C) not all members are able to attain profitable output levels.

    (D) it is more profitable for the industry to charge a lower price and produce more output.

    (E) entry barriers are insignificant in oligopolistic industries.

52. In the United States, professional football players earn much higher incomes than professional hockey players. This is because

    (A) most football players would be good hockey players while the reverse is not true.

(B) consumers have a greater demand for football games than for hockey games.

(C) there is a high degree of substitution of football for hockey games for most consumers.

(D) the total productivity of hockey players exceeds that of football players.

(E) most hockey players are foreign-born.

53. Assume the Tutta Bulla restaurant is hiring labor in an amount such that the MRC of the last worker is $18 and the MRP is $22. On the basis of this information, we can say that

(A) profits will be increased by hiring additional workers.

(B) profits will be increased by hiring fewer workers.

(C) marginal revenue product must exceed average revenue product.

(D) Tutta Bulla is maximizing profits.

(E) Tutta Bulla is operating below minimum AVC.

Answer question 54 on the basis of the following marginal product data for resources A and B. The output of these resources sells in a purely competitive market at $1 per unit.

Inputs of A	MP_A	Inputs of B	MP_B
1	25	1	40
2	20	2	36
3	15	3	32
4	10	4	24
5	5	5	20
6	2	6	16
7	1	7	8

54. Refer to the preceding data. Assuming that the prices of resources A and B are $5 and $8 respectively, what is the profit-maximizing combination of resources?

    (A) 7 of A and 7 of B

    (B) 6 of A and 4 of B

    (C) 5 of A and 7 of B

    (D) 4 of A and 4 of B

    (E) 3 of A and 5 of B

Answer question 55 on the basis of the following data.

Quantity of Labor	MP of Labor	MRP of Labor	Quantity of Capital	MP of Capital	MRP of Capital
1	15	$45	1	8	$24
2	12	36	2	6	18
3	9	27	3	5	15
4	6	18	4	4	12
5	3	9	5	3	9
6	1	3	6	2	6

55. Refer to the preceding data. This firm is selling its product in

    (A) an imperfectly competitive market at prices that decline as sales increase.

    (B) a purely competitive market at $3 per unit.

    (C) a purely competitive market at $2 per unit.

    (D) a pure monopoly at $4 per unit.

    (E) an imperfectly competitive market at $3 per unit.

Pollution Levels

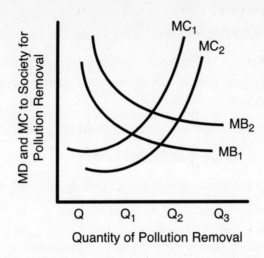

Quantity of Pollution Removal

56. Refer to the preceding diagram. Which of the following might shift the marginal benefit curve from MB_1 to MB_2?

(A) A new government tax on pollution

(B) Major new studies strongly linking cancer to pollution

(C) Improved technology for reducing pollution

(D) A change in consumer tastes for manufacturing goods

(E) A decrease in the price of recycled goods

57. There is little incentive for a firm in a competitive environment to internalize spillover costs, as this would

(A) cause it to forgo the diseconomies of agglomeration.

(B) shift its cost curves downward.

(C) put it at a competitive disadvantage compared to rival producers.

(D) make it subject to emission or effluent fees.

(E) shift its supply curve rightward.

58. In the used car market, new government regulation increasing car quality standards would

    (A) reduce the demand for, and price of, used vehicles.

    (B) give owners of "lemons" more incentive than owners of high-quality new cars to sell their cars, because buyers refuse to pay high prices for "lemons."

    (C) increase demand for used cars, and keep their prices low.

    (D) increase the price and reduce the supply of used cars.

    (E) reduce the price of new cars, because demand would decrease.

59. With respect to the overall impact of progressive taxes and transfer payments on the distribution of income, it can be said that

    (A) taxes decrease, but transfers increase, income inequality.

    (B) taxes increase, but transfers reduce, income inequality.

    (C) both taxes and transfers decrease income inequality.

    (D) both taxes and transfers increase income inequality.

    (E) None of the above.

60. Differences in education and training

    (A) combine with differences in mental, physical, and inherited assets to produce income inequality.

    (B) contribute little to income inequality in the United States.

    (C) explain nearly all the income inequality in the United States.

    (D) explain most, but not all, of the declining income inequality in the United States.

    (E) were ignored as a key element of U.S. quota and affirmative action programs.

AP Microeconomics

Test

Section II

PLANNING TIME: 10 minutes
WRITING TIME: 50 minutes

DIRECTIONS: You have fifty minutes to answer all three of the following questions. It is suggested that you spend approximately half
your time on the first question and divide the remaining time equally
between the next two questions. In answering these questions, you
should emphasize the line of reasoning that generated your results;
it is not enough to list the results of your analysis. Include correctly
labeled diagrams, if useful or required, in explaining your answers. A
correctly labeled diagram must have all axes and curves labeled and
must show directional changes.

Pure Competitive Market

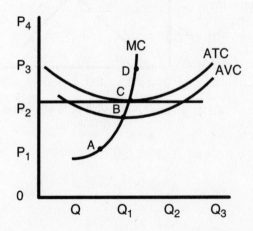

1. The preceding model shows the revenue and cost curves for a purely competitive firm.

    (a) How does the purely competitive firm determine its profit-maximizing level of output and price?

    (b) Identify each of the following items for a purely competitive firm.

        (i)   The profit-maximizing level of output and price

        (ii) The degree of elasticity of the demand for this firm's good

    (c) Where does productive efficiency occur, if at all?

    (d) Where does allocative efficiency occur, if at all?

    (e) Suppose that the industry depicted in the model above became imperfectly competitive and that the industry had an elastic, downward-sloping demand curve. Identify the new equilibrium price and quantity.

        (i)   Identify any price and quantity difference between the two types of firms.

        (ii) Would productive and allocative efficiency be maintained?

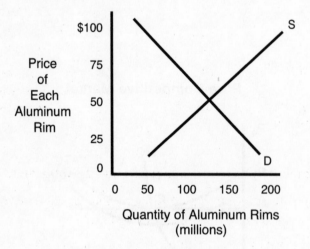

2. During the production of aluminum rims for a new sports car, spillover costs occur in the form of air pollution.

    (a) Congress proposes that a sales tax be levied on each aluminum rim to cover the spillover cost. Explain the effect of this tax upon the following (4 points total):

        (i) The cost of aluminum rims

        (ii) The price paid by consumers for sports cars with aluminum rims

        (iii) The quantity of aluminum rims produced

    (b) Discuss the impact of this tax on the MB = MC analysis of allocative efficiency. (2 points)

3. Assume that a firm produces output by employing labor and capital with the following marginal product combinations. The cost of labor is $25 per input unit and the cost of capital is $120 per input unit. The entire output of these independent resources sells for $5 per unit.

Input of Labor	MP Labor	Inputs of Capital	MP Capital
1	25	1	40
2	20	2	36
3	15	3	32
4	10	4	24
5	5	5	20
6	2	6	16
7	1	7	8

    (a) Employ MRP analysis to determine the following.

        (i) What combination of labor and capital determines maximum profit/minimum loss?

        (ii) What output will this firm produce?

        (iii) Determine this firm's short-run profit or loss.

    (b) If the cost of labor drops to $10 per unit and capital increases to $180 per unit, what changes, if any, will this firm make?

AP Economics

Microeconomics Test

ANSWER KEY

Section I

1.	(C)	16.	(C)	31.	(C)	46.	(C)
2.	(C)	17.	(A)	32.	(E)	47.	(B)
3.	(A)	18.	(B)	33.	(D)	48.	(D)
4.	(C)	19.	(C)	34.	(C)	49.	(B)
5.	(C)	20.	(E)	35.	(D)	50.	(E)
6.	(C)	21.	(A)	36.	(A)	51.	(B)
7.	(D)	22.	(B)	37.	(B)	52.	(B)
8.	(C)	23.	(A)	38.	(B)	53.	(A)
9.	(B)	24.	(B)	39.	(C)	54.	(C)
10.	(E)	25.	(D)	40.	(A)	55.	(B)
11.	(B)	26.	(D)	41.	(A)	56.	(B)
12.	(B)	27.	(B)	42.	(C)	57.	(C)
13.	(E)	28.	(D)	43.	(A)	58.	(D)
14.	(E)	29.	(B)	44.	(C)	59.	(C)
15.	(E)	30.	(E)	45.	(B)	60.	(A)

DETAILED EXPLANATIONS OF ANSWERS

Microeconomics Test

Section I

1.   **(C)**   Microeconomics is primarily focused on the components that make up the economy. In a free-market system, consumers, producers, government, and trade are the four main components.

2.   **(C)**   Economic efficiency is related to the average total cost of producing a good or providing a service. By extracting the maximum production from inputs, we realize minimum average total cost. This productive efficiency, when combined with allocative efficiency, contributes to the realization of the highest standard of living attainable for a society.

3.   **(A)**   The PPF curve is a model that demonstrates the economic reality that all inputs are not equal. It further demonstrates that we have choices in how our resources are employed in the production of alternative goods. In fact, as we exhaust our inputs they diminish in their productive capability, reducing at some point our total productivity, thereby raising our costs.

4.   **(C)**   As discussed in question 3, opportunity cost is the realization that scarcity causes us to make economic choices in how our limited resources are employed in production of alternative goods. As we choose to make one good, we sacrifice the value of the alternative choice.

5.   **(C)**   Box C represents the producer of goods and services that are brought (4) to product market D, and offered for sale to household A.

6.   **(C)**   Critical to the effectiveness of markets is that sellers of similar g/s are in competition for consumer expenditures. "Substitution"

is the word employed by economists to describe the market reality that consumers are willing to replace a good or service whose price has increased with a like g/s.

7.   **(D)**   This is predicated upon the cross-elasticity formula. This formula states that as the price of a g/s decreases and the consumption of another g/s increases a degree of complement exists. Some students are tempted to conclude that C is a correct answer, but income change is not present and is necessary to conclude whether a g/s is inferior or normal/superior.

8.   **(C)**   A basic principle of demand is that price change causes a change in quantity demanded. Price up, Q_d down. Price down, Q_d up. The determinants of demand cause a shift in the demand curve. Be wary of this simple but effective trap!

9.   **(B)**   An increase in the costs of production inputs is a determinant of supply that causes the supply curve to move up and inward, representing higher overall prices. As prices rise, consumers will seek a substitute g/s. Since wine can be substituted for beer and its price has remained constant, consumers will shift some of their expenditure to wine.

10.   **(E)**   The equilibrium (market) price is the intersection point of the supply and demand curves. Trace the equilibrium point to the y-axis and a price of $2.50 is revealed. Trace the equilibrium point to the x-axis and a quantity of 250 gallons is revealed.

11.   **(B)**   A fundamental principle established by Adam Smith was the power of specialization, not only of individuals but nations as well. Specialization results in maximum output from resources, and contributes to economic efficiency, thus minimizing cost.

12.   **(B)**   This answer is based upon the least cost combination of labor and capital. We do not know the marginal product of labor and capital. All we do know is the various combinations of labor and capital that together yield 30 units of output, and the cost of each unit resource. So, by establishing the cost of the four various techniques, we can determine which is the least costly and when subtracted from our total revenue, $(30 \times 0.50 =)$ $15, yields the highest profit. The outcome of the four techniques can be viewed below.

Technique I, 4 labor ($8) + 2 capital ($6) =
$14 and a profit of $1.

Technique II, 3 labor ($6) + 3 capital ($9) =
$15 and 0 profit.

Technique III, 2 labor ($4) + 5 capital ($15) =
$19 and a $4 loss.

Technique IV, 5 labor ($10) + 1 capital ($3) =
$13 and $2 economic profit.

13. **(E)**   This answer combines cross-elasticity of income, consumer behavior and its impact on market forces, and the reaction of
firms to profit. If consumer income increases, the demand for normal
goods would increase. The resultant shift in demand would cause an
increase in equilibrium price and quantity. The higher price and quantity would attract firms to the opportunity to obtain profit.

14. **(E)**   Public goods (like a park or defense) are defined as g/s
that are not divisible and are subject to free riders. Since division of
the g/s is difficult, if not impossible, the incentive of profit is not
present. Therefore, even though the demand for the g/s is clearly
present, it would not be produced in a free market, as profit is not
present and allocative efficiency cannot be determined.

15. **(E)**   The simple price elasticity test determines the percentage
of change in quantity demanded (0.20) divided by the percentage of
change in price (0.10). If the quotient (2) is greater than 1, the demand
is considered elastic. If the quotient is less than 1, it is classified as
inelastic. This measurement tells firms how price-sensitive consumers
are. The total revenue test would work as well; if total revenue goes
up, the demand is elastic, and if the total revenue decreases, the demand is inelastic.

16. **(C)**   This answer is based upon the cross-elasticity of demand
formula. If the price of X goes up (+) and the demand for Y goes down
(–), a negative quotient results, indicating a complementary relationship. If a positive quotient results, the g/s are substitutes, and if there is
no change, the g/s are not related.

17. **(A)**   The formula for cross-elasticity of income determines the
percentage of change in quantity of good X divided by the percentage

of change in the income of the consumer. If the quotient is positive, then the goods are considered normal/superior as the consumer chooses to buy more (as he or she can afford more). If income rises and the consumer buys less, the good is deemed inferior, as the consumer shifts his or her consumption to a superior comparative good.

18. **(B)** Marginal utility measures the change in total utility divided by the change in quantity. In this case, there is a change in total utility from 30 to 36, a change of 6. When divided by the quantity change of 1 (2 to 3 units = 1 unit), the marginal utility quotient is 6.

19. **(C)** This question requires the formula used to determine utility maximization of income, which determines the utility per dollar gained by the purchase of different goods when constrained by an income budget. This formula seeks to find a balance in satisfaction, as consumers do, when choosing the combination of goods to purchase within their limited income. The formula is $MU_X/P_X = MU_Y/P_Y =$ budget \$. So, divide the MU at each quantity by the price of that good to obtain the MU per dollar of that good. When the MU per dollar of two or more goods is equal, and the combined quantity purchased is within the budget constraint, you have utility maximization. In this case, at 4 units of X you have a per dollar MU of 3 (24/\$8 = 3), and at 5 units of Y you have an MU per dollar of 3 (12/\$4 = 3), so the utils per dollar are equal. The next step is to determine if this combination of goods is within the budget constraints. 4 units of X × \$8 each = \$32 spent, and 5 units of Y × \$4 each = \$20 spent, for a total of \$52. MU per dollar of X = 3, MU per dollar of Y = 3 = \$52 budget.

20. **(E)** This answer is predicated upon the utility-maximizing formula established in the previous question. As you increase the quantity purchased at a fixed price, the utility per dollar decreases. For example, if good X costs \$2 per unit, and you increase your purchasing by one unit while MU decreases from 20 to 10, your per dollar MU would also decrease from 10 (20MU/\$2) to 5 (10MU/\$2).

21. **(A)** Economists determine costs and profits differently than accountants. An accountant views a firm's costs as consisting only of explicit (out of pocket) expenses, thus to them profit is total revenue (price × quantity) minus fixed and variable costs. The economist, however, includes implicit costs, like the lost value of alternative uses for startup capital, as well as entrepreneurial value (normal profit). So, breakeven point for an accountant would, to an economist, occur dur-

ing economic loss, and when the economist observes breakeven point (includes normal profit) the accountant would see profit.

22. **(B)**   This is a simple definition question. Short run is the length of time during which at least one input is fixed (plant size). Do not confuse this with increased or decreased utilization of existing plant size (24 hour, 7 day use) or shutdown of existing plants.

23. **(A)**   This is another simple definition question. Marginal product formula is the change in total output divided by the change in input.

24. **(B)**   This is a definition question. Even if we assume that all worker inputs are equal, at some point the relationship between the number of workers and the fixed plant (overcrowding) would result in inefficiencies that would cause the total product to decline. This realization is critical to understanding the shape of production cost curves.

25. **(D)**   This answer is based upon the formula for determining marginal product. The change in total output divided by the change in input equals the marginal product. In this case, the change from 5 inputs to 6 inputs = 1 and total product increases from 165 to 180 = 15. 15 divided by 1 = a marginal product of 15.

26. **(D)**   The formula from question 25, when applied to the relationship between increasing inputs and total productivity (opportunity costs increase, input quality diminishes as it is exhausted), yields the economic reality that at some point, the inputs of production will actually decrease total productivity, causing marginal productivity to become negative.

27. **(B)**   By definition, insurance is a set premium that does not vary with a fixed farm size.

28. **(D)**   Variable costs are defined as those costs that change as production increases or decreases. Fixed costs do not vary as output varies within a fixed plant structure. If the fixed plant changes in the long run production process, fixed costs can increase or decrease, but then will become fixed at new levels.

29. **(B)**   By definition, marginal cost is the change in the total cost divided by the change in quantity produced.

30. **(E)**   By definition, AFC is the fixed cost divided by the total quantity produced. Mathematically, this number would constantly decline to infinity but the rate of decline would increasingly diminish.

31. **(C)**   By definition, ATC = AFC + AVC. Therefore, ATC – AVC = AFC. This is the graphic model of this algebraic statement.

32. **(E)**   Technical advance, by definition, means an improvement in the efficiency of output, i.e., you get more output from less input. Since costs are the inverse of productivity, as productivity increases, costs decrease, and A through D are all costs that would decrease if a technical advance increased productivity. Graphically, lower costs are represented by the curves moving downward towards the x-axis.

33. **(D)**   By definition, fixed costs are constant, so the change in total variable cost between two different outputs would determine the change in total cost. Output × AVC = TVC. At 6 units, our total variable cost is 6 × $73.33 = $439.98. At 7 units of production, our total variable costs would be 7 × $80.00 = $560.00. The change in total cost caused by the increase in output from 6 to 7 units is $560.00 – 439.98 = $120.02.

34. **(C)**   Profit equals total revenue minus total cost, and the given mission of this firm is to produce at the maximum profit in the short run.

35. **(D)**   This answer requires knowledge of the basic definitions of breakeven and normal profit. Breakeven is the quantity and price combination wherein a firm's ATC = (average) price per unit sold. To an economist, normal profit would be included in ATC as an implicit cost of doing business, as noted earlier.

36. **(A)**   Marginal revenue = marginal cost is a basic tenet of all firm behavior in any environment. The assumption is that all firms seek short run maximization of profit or minimization of loss. These profit/loss points always occur where MR = MC. If MR > MC, more profit (or less loss) could be had by increasing output. If MR < MC, more loss could be avoided (or profit might be obtained) by reducing output.

37. **(B)**   This table verifies the MR = MC rule discussed previously. At output quantity 3, we come closest to MR = MC, and thus

maximum profit. By adding MR at each level of output, we obtain total revenue of $48.00 with a total cost of $10 + 9 + 13 = $32.00, for a profit of $16.00. Any other output has less profit. At output quantity 4, output level TR is $64.00 and TC is $49.00, for a profit of $15.00—in other words, profits are not maximized as they are at MR = MC.

38. **(B)** At price 2, average price per product equals average variable cost. The firm is experiencing economic loss and its fixed and implicit costs are not being covered. However, its variable costs are being covered at this revenue level. A firm can continue to operate, in the short run, as long as inputs of production (like its workers) are being paid. It can keep the doors open in the hope that other firms will exit the market. If firms exit the market, prices would rise as industry supply decreased, and breakeven would be attained. Remember, in a purely competitive market, P = D = MR and is perfectly elastic for the individual firm, which is a price taker. But the entire industry does have a downward sloping demand curve. So, as firms exit, the Industry Supply would shift left and price would rise in the industry, and to each individual firm.

39. **(C)** This question uses the MR = MC formula for profit maximization. If MR is $42, then this firm would produce at the 10 output level, where MC is $41 ($42 = $41). At 10 units, Total Revenue = $420.00 and Total Cost = 10 × (ATC) 31.60 = $316.00. TR – TC = profit, so $420.00 – $316.00 = $104.

40. **(A)** By definition, short-run shutdown point occurs where revenue does not cover the variable cost. If the workers are not paid, they will not work. If vendors are not paid, they don't deliver production resources. This soon results in the firm going out of business.

41. **(A)** By definition, marginal cost is the change in total cost/ change in output. At output 4, TC is $270; at output 5, TC is $350. The change is $80/output change of 1 = MC = $80.

42. **(C)** Firms are attracted to economic profit, repelled by loss, and constant if at normal profit. So an industry would expand if existing firms were enjoying economic profit. Firms would enter until the industry returned to normal profit levels.

43. **(A)** A firm attains least cost maximum profit/minimum loss, where MR = MC. Since this firm is producing at an output where MR

< MC, by reducing output, it would increase MR, decrease MC, and improve its profit/loss position.

44. **(C)** In a purely competitive industry, productive efficiency (least costly) occurs where the price (which represents society's marginal benefit) quantity combination intersects minimum ATC, indicating lowest-cost production quantity. When quantity produced results in an intersection of price and marginal cost, allocative efficiency (quantity of goods most wanted by society) results. If price (MB) is greater than MC, underallocation of resources is occurring (increase production). If price (MB) is less than MC, then overallocation of resources is occurring (cut production).

45. **(B)** This firm is overproducing and overallocating resources, as Q_2 results in an ATC greater than revenue. Neither productive nor allocative efficiency is occurring; in fact, this firm has economic loss. Under these market conditions, the firm should reduce output to a Q_1 level and return to normal profit.

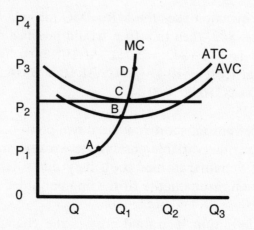

46. **(C)** By definition, public goods are indivisible and subject to free ridership, since price can't be used to determine use. Since profit cannot be obtained, there is no incentive to produce; at best, they would be underproduced.

47. **(B)** Firms maximize/minimize profits where MR = MC. MR = MC at quantity E and Price A. This firm will enjoy maximum economic profit at this price/demand and quantity.

48. **(D)** Pure monopolies produce a quantity that results in a price that underallocates resources, since the total revenue generated by doing this results in the highest profit margin.

49. **(B)** In long-run equilibrium, a monopolistically competitive firm can, at best, maintain normal profit, which occurs when MR = MC and price equals minimum ATC. If price rose above minimum ATC, economic profit would result, and firms would be attracted to the industry. If price fell below minimum ATC, economic loss would cause firms to exit the industry until equilibrium was attained.

50. **(E)** Due to ease of entrance and exit, as well as high levels of competition present in this market model, economic profit attracts firms, and economic loss repels firms until long run equilibrium occurs, when price/quantity equals minimum ATC.

51. **(B)** Cartels are oligopolies acting in collusion that obtain monopoly status through their use of quotas to control quantity produced. High prices and economic profits are attained as a result. By secretly cheating on their cartel partners, they obtain the higher prices and increase their share of the economic profit. This is successful only in the short run, since in the long run prices would fall due to increased output and (assumed) constant demand. As cartel members realized that members were cheating, they would return to competition and the cartel would cease to function.

52. **(B)** Wages are the result of derived demand. Assume that the supply of two goods (sports entertainment) is equal. If the demand for one sport is greater than the other, the price paid for the good would be higher. This reflects in the cost of the inputs to the producer in the labor market for football and hockey players.

53. **(A)** Comparing Marginal Revenue Product and Marginal Resource Cost (MRP = MRC) is another method of determining maximum profit (similar to MR = MC concept), this time by balancing the marginal cost of resource inputs to the marginal revenue those resources generate for the firm. In the case of Tutta Bulla, the revenue generated at this level of output, while profitable, is not maximum profit. By producing more units, the marginal cost will rise, yet profits will also grow until MRP = MRC.

54. **(C)** This question employs the formulas introduced in question 53. However, an additional formula has been added. In this case, it is necessary to balance the Marginal Productivity of two different inputs of production (labor and capital, for instance) with the marginal revenue they generate at various output levels. The formula is stated as MPA/price of A = MPB/price of B = marginal revenue product. Therefore, at units of A, 5 (MP)/$5 (5 units × $1 each) equals 7 units of B 8 (MP)/$8 (8 units × $1 each) = 1 = MRP of 1.

55. **(B)** This is another method of testing your knowledge of the MRP formula, and combines it with knowledge of price structure of firms in different competitive market structures. Since MRP of labor = MP of labor × price of each unit produced, at 1 unit of labor MRP = 15 × $x = $45. Therefore, x = $3 price per unit. This quotient is the same at all output levels of labor. It is also true for the MP of capital and MRP of capital. 1 unit of capital has an MP of 8 units, so MRP = 8 × $x = $24; x = $3 price per unit. Since the price of each unit of production remains at $3, no matter the level of output, it must be a firm in a purely competitive market. Only in the purely competitive market is price perfectly inelastic and equal to marginal revenue.

56. **(B)** Marginal Benefit reflects society's overall satisfaction with a g/s at various price quantity combinations—in this case, clean air and water. Marginal Cost is the cost of producing that clean air and water in those various combinations. So, as in all other free markets, equilibrium occurs when the cost of supplying clean air and water equals society's willingness to pay that price quantity combination. A change in MB is, in essence, an increase in demand for clean air and water. Only answer (B) would stimulate an increase in the demand for clean air and water. Since the demand would increase, quantity supplied would increase, and the price paid by society would rise.

57. **(C)** A spillover cost is a cost of production not borne directly by the producer or the consumer of a g/s. Society bears that cost, as in air pollution—if a firm in a competitive industry chose to bear the cost of pollution, its profits would diminish or it would have to raise its price. Since rival firms would not lose profits or have to raise their price (consumers would substitute the cheaper g/s), they would grow in strength.

58. **(D)** Again, this question concerns the impact that government intervention, in the form of taxation or regulation, has on a firm's cost

structure, and thus market equilibrium. If government required sellers of used cars to guarantee higher reliability requirements, this would increase the cost of supplying cars to the consumer. These higher over-all costs would shift the supply curve up and to the left. The resultant new market equilibrium would be at a higher price, with few cars demanded and supplied.

59. **(C)**   Both progressive taxes and transfer payments, by defini-tion, collect money from higher incomes and redistribute that money to lower incomes. Especially in the case of an increasing marginal in-come tax (the more one earns, the greater the percentage of tax) these are income-leveling activities.

60. **(A)**   Derived demand significantly determines labor prices in a free-labor market. Differences in education and training make a worker more productive (MRP) and/or increasingly scarce (MRC). When a tight supply of highly skilled labor is combined with a high demand for that worker, a high price is paid. Since income is a great determinant of wealth, these factors in a free labor market would contribute to income inequality.

DETAILED EXPLANATIONS
OF ANSWERS

Microeconomics Test

Section II

1. (a)   All firms operate employing the MR = MC model as the least-cost combination, maximum profit/minimum loss rule. When employing this axiom (regarding profit to a firm in a perfectly competitive environment), we must additionally realize that the firm is a "price taker"—in other words, although there is a downward sloping demand curve for the entire industry, in a perfectly competitive market, no one firm has enough of a market share to influence the price. Since price equals both demand and marginal revenue for the firm, the best it can hope for in the long run is to operate at a point where price is equal to minimum ATC. This would represent maximum profit, which in this case would be defined as a point of normal profit. (1 point)

   (b)   (i)   The profit-maximizing level for the purely competitive firm depicted by the given model is the equilibrium point C and P_3 price – Q_1 quantity. (1 point)

   (ii)   As stated in (a), for a purely competitive firm, price is perfectly elastic. The assumption is that this firm can sell all it makes at one price. This is why price = demand = marginal revenue in the perfectly competitive model. (1 point)

   (c)   Productive efficiency does occur, where price intersects minimum ATC. This point, C, represents the firm maximizing its use of resource inputs (achieving the greatest output per resource input).

Thus, the least cost per unit of output is expended. Any other production output quantity results in a higher cost per unit. (1 point)

(d) Allocative efficiency is different from productive efficiency in that it does not assume least cost production, but rather the output number of goods which best benefits society. Remember that price is the consumer's communication to producers regarding the marginal benefit (utility) derived from the product. Allocative efficiency (P = MC) occurs when the price (marginal benefit) of a good equals its marginal cost. If price equals marginal cost at minimum ATC, then allocative efficiency would occur along with productive efficiency. Note that if price were greater than MC, the consumer would indicate to the industry that they were underallocating resources through the higher market price. Since there would be short-run profits in this industry, firms would flock to it until it returned to long-run equilibrium at normal profit. If price were less than marginal cost, the consumer would indicate to producers that the industry was overallocating resources to this good. Firms would be operating at economic loss in short-run equilibrium. The industry would adjust to these market conditions by firms exiting the industry until long-run equilibrium returned to normal profit prices. (1 point)

(e)

Imperfectly Competitive Market Model

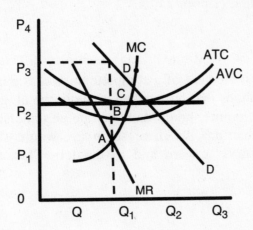

The new price and quantity equilibrium would be the result of the change to a pure monopoly. The maximum profit rule of MR = MC (point A) would still apply. Notice that a monopoly is able to create a higher price (P_4) in the market by producing at a quantity below mini-mum (ATC Q_1) and far below Marginal Benefit to society (Q_1). Where MR = MC for the pure monopoly, neither productive nor allocative efficiency is attained. This control of output ("price maker") relative to demand allows the pure monopoly to achieve long run economic profit. Pure monopoly is the only firm that can do this. (1 point)

(i)   Purely competitive firms ("price takers") seek, by exit and entrance from an industry, a price (marginal rev-enue / quantity equilibrium) where normal profit is achieved (P_3 and Q_1 in this model).

Imperfect Competition seeks to employ its control (they restrict output) of market output ("price maker") to create an equilibrium where the market is underserved, and maximum economic profit occurs. Monopolies can incur economic loss if the demand curve for their product is below the ATC curve. (1 point)

(ii)   As indicated in prior rationale, purely competitive firms can attain long-run productive and allocative ef-ficiency. Imperfect competition manufactures eco-nomic profit by operating at prices and quantities at which neither productive nor allocative efficiency oc-curs. (1 point)

2.   (a)   The first element of a complete answer is a new graph dem-onstrating the changes that have taken place in the aluminum rim mar-ket. The model (1 point) should demonstrate an understanding that tax is a cost of production. An increase in tax would shift the supply (marginal cost) curve upward and to the left. This would alter the equilibrium point.

Aluminum Rim Market

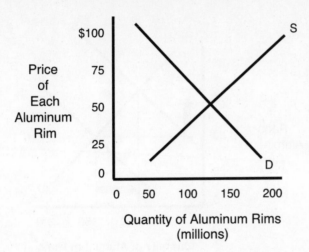

(i) The cost of aluminum rims would increase due to the imposed tax on rims. (1 point)

(ii) The price paid for sports cars with aluminum rims should also increase by $100 ($25 × 4 rims). However, producers might choose not to pass the additional cost of the rims on to consumers. Producers, at times, will absorb a rise in costs, depending upon their margin of profit, the impact a higher price might have upon consumers' demand, and product differentiation (degree of industry competition). (1 point)

(iii) The quantity of aluminum rims consumed will decrease from 150 million to 100 million. Remember the law of demand: as price increases, the quantity demanded declines. (1 point)

Aluminum Rim Market

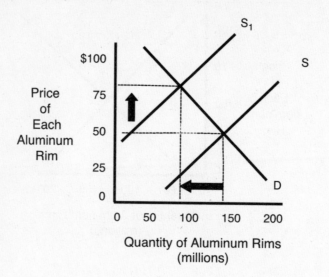

Quantity of Aluminum Rims
(millions)

(b)   The MB = MC concept is a way to view the conflict that arises in a free market economy as we struggle with the overall societal satisfaction from a g/s relative to its cost. It is important to note that initially MB = MC was resulting in allocative efficiency; however, the true cost of the aluminum rims was not reflected in the market, as air quality (market failure) was unaccounted for. The producer's supply curve understates the total cost of production. Since the price of air pollution is passed on to society as a whole, the firm enjoys lower production costs and greater profit. Once the true cost to society is factored in, society's optimal amount of air pollution reduction will occur at the new market equilibrium. Does this mean that society will rid itself of all pollution by imposing sales tax? Not at all, for air quality also has a diminishing marginal utility as well. The added benefit of ever-cleaner air will at some point be exceeded by the added cost, thereby reducing society's net well-being.

3.

Input of Labor	MP Labor	TP	Total Revenue	MR of Labor	Inputs of Capital	MP Capital	TP	Total Revenue	MRP of Capital
1	25	25	$125	$125	1	40	40	$200	$200
2	20	45	225	100	2	36	76	380	180
3	15	60	300	75	3	32	108	540	160
4	10	70	350	50	4	24	132	660	**120**
5	5	75	375	**25**	5	20	152	760	100
6	2	77	385	10	6	16	168	840	80
7	1	78	390	5	7	8	174	870	30

(a) Employing MRP analysis, it is determined:

(i) The following formula illustrates the combination of labor and capital determining maximum profit/minimum loss:

$$\frac{\text{MRP of Labor}}{\text{Price of Labor}} = \frac{\text{MRP of Capital}}{\text{Price of Capital}} = 1$$

At 5 units of labor we have MRP 25/$25 = 1, and at 4 units of capital we have MRP 120/$120 = 1. Therefore, our firm will maximize profits with this least-cost combination of resources.

(ii) At 5 units of labor producing 75 outputs, and 4 units of capital producing 132, the sum (75 + 132 = 207 units) will be produced and sold.

(iii) Our Total Revenue at this combination is (75 × $5) + (132 × $5) = $375 + $660 = $1035. Our Total Cost at this combination is (5 labor × $25) + (4 capital × $120) = $125 + $480 = $605. The firm's profit is $1,035 − $605 = $430.

(b)   Since the price of labor declined while the cost of capital increased, a new least-cost profit maximizing combination will arise. The firm will hire 1 more worker, for a total of 6, and reduce its capital employment from 4 units to 2 resource units. This would also alter its maximum profit. Total Revenue is $765 (labor TP 77 + capital TP 76 = an output of 153; 153 × $5 = $765). Total Cost is $420 (6 labor × $10 = $60 and 2 capital × $180 = $360; $60 + $360 = $420). The profit, $345, is calculated by subtracting the Total Cost from the Total Revenue ($765 – $420 = $345).

MACROECONOMICS REVIEW

AP MACROECONOMICS COURSE STRUCTURE

MACROECONOMICS: BASIC ECONOMIC CONCEPTS

A macroeconomics course introduces students to fundamental economic concepts such as scarcity and opportunity costs. Students will study comparative advantage to determine the basis on which mutually advantageous trade can take place between countries and to identify comparative advantage from differences in output levels and labor costs. Other basic concepts that are explored include the functions performed by an economic system and the way the tools of supply and demand can be used to analyze a market economy. Coverage of these concepts provides students with the foundation for a thorough understanding of macroeconomics and puts the macroeconomic material of the course in proper perspective.

MEASUREMENT OF ECONOMIC PERFORMANCE

The performance of the economy as a whole is usually measured by trends in gross national product, gross domestic product, inflation, and unemployment. Thus, an effective AP course is structured around these important concepts. The course covers the components of gross income measures and the costs of inflation and unemployment. It clarifies the important distinction between nominal and real values, and gives students some exposure to the use of price indices to convert nominal magnitudes into real magnitudes. Students learn how the unemployment rate is measured and consider the seeming paradox of a positive unemployment rate when there is so-called full employment. As the course moves from mere static descriptions to dynamic models, it considers the actual levels of U.S. inflation, unemployment, gross national product, and gross domestic product, as well as the ways that changes in one may affect the others.

NATIONAL INCOME AND PRICE DETERMINATION

Analysis of the determination of national income and of the aggregate price level is the core of a well-planned AP macroeconomics course. This analysis often begins with a general discussion of the nature and shape of the aggregate demand and supply curves. The course can then present the differences between the Keynesian and Classical views of the shape of the aggregate supply curve and the importance of the shape in determining the effect of changes in aggregate demand on the economy. Once students grasp the traditional Keynesian and Classical views, they are ready to consider alternative views held by macroeconomists on the shape of the aggregate supply curve.

A detailed study of aggregate demand may begin with an outline of the circular flow of goods and earnings in the economy. The basic Keynesian expenditure model can be used to identify the total spending/output equilibrium and to demonstrate the importance of the spending multiplier concept. By including an investigation of the effect of government fiscal policy on aggregate demand, the course requires students to examine the differing effects of discretionary tax and expenditure policies, and to discuss the role of automatic stabilizers.

An important step in analyzing aggregate demand is the study of the effect of monetary policy. Here, the course introduces students to the definition of money, fractional reserve banking, and the Federal Reserve System. It is also appropriate for the teacher to introduce the topics of multiple-deposit expansion and money creation, and to discuss the tools of monetary policy. In learning about monetary policy, students find it helpful to define the determinants of the demand for money. From a study of these determinants, they can proceed to investigate how equilibrium in the money market determines interest rates, how the investment demand curve provides the link between changes in the money market and changes in aggregate demand, and how changes in aggregate demand affect the money market.

With both monetary and fiscal policies now incorporated in the analysis of aggregate demand, an understanding of the interaction between the two is essential. Some knowledge of the concepts of "crowding out" and accommodating monetary policy is important, as is some acquaintance with the issues dividing the monetarists and traditional Keynesians. After gaining an understanding of the monetarist and Keynesian views of macroeconomics, students are ready to analyze other theories of macroeconomic behavior. In their study of the proper mix between monetary and fiscal policies, students should examine the economic effects of government budget deficits, consider the issues involved in determining the burden of the national debt, and explore the relationships between deficits, interest rates, and inflation.

Having covered aggregate demand in detail, the course can now present the aggregate supply curve. It is important for students to understand why many economists believe that this curve may be upward-sloping in the short run but vertical in the long run. With this understanding, students can distinguish between the short-run and long-run impacts of monetary and fiscal policies and trace the short-run and long-run effects of supply shocks. Short-run and long-run Phillips curves can be introduced to help students gain an understanding of the inflation-unemployment trade-off and how this trade-off may differ in the short and long run. A well-rounded course also includes an examination of inflationary expectations and an analysis of how disagreements over both the cause and rate of change of these expectations separate traditional Keynesians and Neo-classical economists.

ECONOMIC GROWTH

Students should understand the contributions of economic growth to job creation and economic well-being. The determinants of economic growth should be emphasized. Furthermore, the impacts of monetary and fiscal policies on the growth of a nation's economy should be studied.

INTERNATIONAL FINANCE, EXCHANGE RATES, AND BALANCE OF PAYMENTS

The formulation of macroeconomic policy has important ramifications for international economics. Students need to understand that the combination of monetary and fiscal policies used in addressing problems of inflation and unemployment has an effect on international factors such as exchange rates and the balance of payments. Students also need to understand the reverse: that international forces, often beyond a country's control, affect a country's exchange rates, which, in turn, affect a country's price level, unemployment, and level of output. It is important to examine what the effects of trade restrictions are, how the international payments system hinders or facilitates trade, how domestic policy actions affect international finance and trade, and how international exchange rates affect domestic policy goals.

MACROECONOMICS REVIEW

KEY TERMS

GDP
Aggregate expenditure
AE model
Inflation
Stagflation
CPI
GDP deflator
Cost-push inflation
Demand-pull inflation
Keynesian theory
Say's Law
Supply side
Demand side
Laffer curve
Phillips curve
Marginal propensity to consume
Marginal propensity to save
Equilibrium GDP
GDP multiplier
Investment demand
AD/AS model
Monetary policy
Fiscal policy
Crowding out
Money supply
Bonds
Federal Reserve System
Banks
Money multiplier
Balance sheet
FOMC
Expansionary policy

Contractionary policy
NAFTA
GATT
WTO
Global economy
Comparative advantage
Absolute advantage
Balance of payments
Fixed or floating exchange rates

Macroeconomics is the study of the overall performance of an economy. Critical to an understanding of macroeconomics is the role of economic indicators. Hundreds of different indicators are available today, all measuring different aspects of our complicated system. We will focus on the key indicators that paint a picture of an economy in broad strokes. These indicators fall into three main categories: leading, coincidental, and lagging. Based on our earlier investigation of the circular flow model, it is easy to understand that the first logical indicator of the state of our economic performance is a measure of the dollar flow of payments for input resources or the output value of goods and services consumed. Each is measured by a different government agency: output by the Department of Commerce, and income by the Internal Revenue Service.

MEASURING ECONOMIC PERFORMANCE

The basic measurement used by economists to gauge the overall state of the economy today is gross domestic product (GDP), defined as the dollar value of all final goods and services produced within the nation's borders within one year. The ownership of the firm is not an issue, only the domestic origin of the good or service. This also explains why the original GNP (gross national product) indicator has been replaced by GDP, as GNP measures g/s produced by U.S. businesses regardless of location. So, a good produced by a British-owned company in the United States would have its production value (excluding profits taken back to Britain) added to GDP but not GNP. By the same token, a good produced in Mexico City by a U.S. company would not be included in GDP (except profits brought back to the United States), but would be counted in GNP. Thus, GDP is the sum of all the money spent purchasing final goods and services produced in the United States, regardless of firm ownership.

Another way to measure economic activity is to measure the income derived or earned by creating those goods and services. Therefore, we can measure productivity by a national income approach or a national expenditure approach; in the end, they should be equal. This is a lagging indicator, in that it measures an event that has already happened.

The expenditure measurement consists of four components: household consumption expenditure (C), gross business domestic investment (Ig), government purchases (G), and net foreign purchases (Xn) (subtract import value, as foreign goods are not a part of U.S. productivity). This can be stated as a simple formula:

C + Ig + G + Xn

The national income measurement totals five main sources of income: wages, salaries, rents, interest, and profits from business ownership (including sole proprietorships, partnerships, and private and public corporations).

One of the key issues in the creation of this indicator is possible change in money value over time; that is, inflation or deflation. Economists deal with this issue by distinguishing between nominal measurement (current dollars) and real measurement (reflecting changes in price levels or constant dollars). If one wants to use GDP in a comparative manner—say, GDP in 1999 compared to the GDP in 2000—real GDP must be used, or any conclusion reached would be flawed.

ECONOMIC PERFORMANCE OVER TIME

Economic growth is an increase in real GDP. Economic contraction is a decrease in real GDP. Total expenditure is the immediate determinant of output, and thus of unemployment/employment and inflation/deflation. The business cycle, depicted in figure 1, is a way of explaining change in aggregate expenditure.

There are five parts to the business cycle:

- Expansion
- Peak
- Contraction (recession)
- Trough (bottom)
- Recovery

Business Cycle

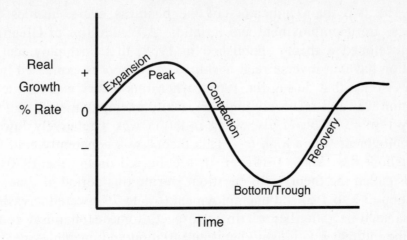

Figure 1

The time and degree of each phase varies. The generally accepted definition of a recession is six months of negative GDP growth. Many things can cause fluctuations in economic expenditure. Some cycle changes result from seasonal change; others are due to technological innovation, political events such as war, money supply and interest rates, or even the degree of household debt. Regardless of the cause, a change in total spending results in a change in total output. Economists try to track and predict these movements by economic indicators. These indicators fall into three categories:

- Leading (predict a change)

- Coincidental (happen at the same time)

- Lagging (after the change)

All three types of indicators are useful. During recession or expansion, g/s experience different rates of change. Goods seem to experience a greater degree of change than services. Durable (lasting longer than three years) and capital goods show a greater degree of change than nondurable goods (lifespan less than three years). Nondurable goods tend to be less expensive and necessary. Durable goods tend to be expensive, somewhat of a luxury, and their purchase is thus more postponable.

PHILLIPS CURVE

The two main indicators of the business cycle, besides GDP change, are unemployment and inflation. A.W. Phillips of Great Britain developed a theory, published in 1958, that unemployment and inflation have an inverse relationship. The concept is expressed in figure 2. Notice that during the 1960s, when this theory was first tested, inflation was at a relatively high 7%, while unemployment was a relatively low 4%. Conversely, when inflation was a relatively low 3%, unemployment was a high 6%. This theory was apparently confirmed throughout the 1960s. However, data collected during the 1970s and 1980s called the theory into question. During this period of time, both inflation (3% to 7%) and unemployment (6% to 7%) were increasing at the same time (stagflation). In retrospect, some economists contend that the indirect relationship between inflation and unemployment was still present but at overall higher levels. The cause of this behavior was cost-push inflation due to the rising price of oil during the energy crises in 1974 and 1980. Also, the very low levels of both inflation and unemployment during the 1990s were most likely due to the increased productivity experienced during this decade. This topic is revisited during discussion of the AD/AS model.

Phillips Curve

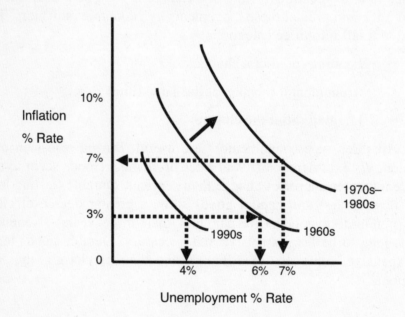

Figure 2

Determining unemployment is relatively simple (*labor force* is defined as the number able and willing to work):

$$\text{unemployment rate} = \frac{\text{unemployed}}{\text{labor force}} \times 100$$

However, using unemployment as an indicator of the state of the economy requires adjustment. There are three types of unemployment:

- structural (mismatch of skills or job location)

- frictional (between jobs)

- cyclical (due to decline in total spending)

Cyclical unemployment gives economists the best picture of the state of the economy. Therefore, to determine cyclical unemployment, the natural rate of unemployment (structural and frictional, which varies over time) must be subtracted from total unemployment. So, full employment in economic terms does not mean 100% employment. If cyclical unemployment were at 0%, we would realize our full production possibility. Government guarantee of full employment is a hotly debated political issue.

CONSUMER PRICE INDEX

Another means to measure the change in value due to changing prices, inflation, or deflation is the Consumer Price Index (CPI). This index is determined much like the GDP deflator except that the household spending pattern is fixed. The formula for the index is:

$$\text{CPI} = \frac{\text{market basket of set g/s for the year to be determined}}{\text{market basket of the same set of g/s for a base}} \times 100$$

This gives the percentage of inflation or deflation present in that year on a constant set of goods. This is a lagging indicator, as it measures an event that has already happened. For example:

1982–1984	100.0 base year
1999	166.6
2000	172.2

The inflation rate for 2000 was 3.4%; (172.2 − 166.6) ÷ 166.6 = 3.4%.

Shortcomings of this approach include:

- changing spending patterns (consumers shift purchases in response to changes in relative prices)

- new products (either not included in basket or weighted improperly)

- quality improvements (leading to greater reliability)

The reality is that the market basket of g/s we purchase changes over time, and the percentage of income spent on a specific g/s may also change. This would result in over- or understating the rate of inflation/deflation. This may prove especially troubling when the CPI is employed by government to adjust transfer payments such as Social Security.

GDP PRICE INDEX

The deflator formula is: Real GDP = Nominal GDP/Price Index (see CPI).

A price index is determined by measuring the price of a basket of g/s in a base year and dividing it by the price of the same basket of goods in the year to be determined, times 100. This percentage of change yields the price index in nominal GDP relative to the index year. Another method is to divide nominal GDP by real GDP, which gives a GDP price index. For example:

Year	Nominal GDP	Real GDP	GDP Price Index
1970	5680.0	6548.0	86.7
1980	7407.2	7407.2	100.0
1990	9864.5	8432.6	117.07

This table establishes 1980 as the base index year and recognizes that nominal GDP in 1970 was undervalued, as the dollar was worth more then than in 1980 or 1990. Thus, 1970 GDP was understated. Conversely, this index would show that nominal GDP in 1990 was overstated, due to inflation that had occurred since the base year.

EFFECTS OF INFLATION

Inflation harms some, helps others, and leaves still others unaffected. Fixed-income recipients (retirees on private pensions or fixed annuities) are harmed by inflation because their spending/income power diminishes. Savers (retirement plans with fixed assets such as bonds) see the relative spending power of their money diminish, and creditors (banks) that have lent money at a fixed rate of return receive repayment in less valuable dollars. Debtors benefit from unanticipated inflation as they pay back loans with cheaper dollars. Individuals or firms that enjoy pricing power may see revenue grow faster than costs rise (real estate values). The effects of deflation are, of course, the opposite of these inflation scenarios.

TYPES OF INFLATION

There are two different types of inflation: cost-push and demand-pull. Cost-push inflation is generally due to an unexpected rise in resource inputs, sometimes termed a "supply shock" by economists. As prices rise in reaction, and quantity demanded decreases, firms produce fewer g/s and lay off workers. Two examples of this type of inflation occurred in 1972–1975 and in 1979–1980. In both instances the rapid increase in energy costs, triggered by OPEC oil price increases, led to reduction in output, higher prices, and increased unemployment. Some economists call this *stagflation*. Resource cost-push inflation is graphed in figure 3.

Cost-Push Inflation

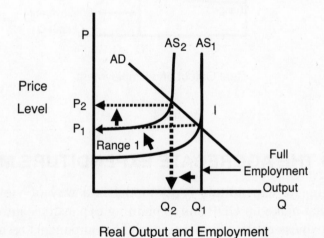

Real Output and Employment

Figure 3

Economists differ on the harm or benefits of mild inflation (less than 3%). Those who claim that any inflation is harmful point to the costs to businesses and households associated with price changes. In contrast, some believe that minor inflation provides a cushion of money necessary to maintaining strong levels of spending, full employment, high profits, and expansion of productivity.

Demand-pull inflation occurs when price levels rise rapidly because of total spending in excess of total productivity. This excess demand quickly bids up the price of available goods. This is often described as too much money pursuing too few goods.

In extreme cases of hyperinflation, as seen in figure 4, panic over increasingly worthless money may throw an economy into a state of barter and unemployment in which economic, social, and political upheaval occurs. Therefore, prevention of hyperinflation is one of the most significant missions of government. However, determining the causes of inflation is difficult, as is finding a cure.

Demand-Pull Inflation

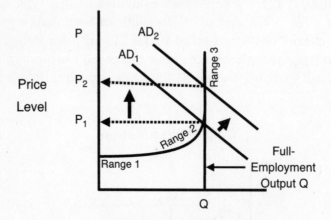

Real Output and Employment

Figure 4

BUILDING THE AGGREGATE EXPENDITURE MODEL

The aggregate expenditure (AE) model is a way of viewing the components that make up GDP and explaining expansions and contractions in the business cycle. An increase in the components results in an increase in GDP. A decrease in a component results in a decrease in

GDP. This way of viewing GDP is sometimes referred to as *leakage and injection*. Knowledge of this concept allows one to influence growth or contraction in the business cycle.

THE GREAT DEBATE

The AE model attacks the foundation of Classical economics as put forth by Say, Ricardo, and Mill. Classical economists denied that a level of spending in an economy could be too low to purchase the entire full employment output. Say's Law, which stated that "supply creates its own demand," acknowledged that short run downturns in the economy, due to geopolitical events like war, were possible. However, when these reductions in AD occurred, there would be an eventual adjustment in lower price, wage, and interest rate levels (figure 5) that would return the economy to full employment. These events would stimulate an expansion in consumer and investment spending, thus increasing AD and leading to a self-correcting view of the business cycle.

Inelastic (Short Run) Supply
Classical Macroeconomic Theory

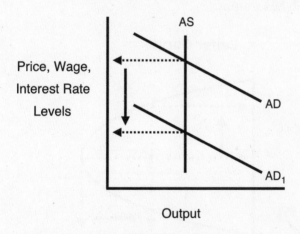

Figure 5

John Maynard Keynes, in his book *General Theory of Employment, Interest, and Money* (1936), developed the AE ideas. He pointed out that not all income need be spent at the time it is produced; in fact, it may be saved. Business investment spending is volatile, and a decline in consumption and investment will cause a decrease in total expenditure. This decline in spending causes a buildup of inventories that producers respond to by firing workers and reducing their output. Furthermore, in stark contrast to the Classical economists' assertions, the resulting recessions are not self-correcting and may continue long-term. In other words, an economy can get "stuck" at a very low level of output. Finally, in direct opposition to the classical "laissez faire" view, Keynes believed that government should play the key role in revitalizing a stagnant economy by stimulating demand. This method of government regulation of the business cycle has come to be called *demand-side economics.*

In the 1980s under President Reagan, some economists united to revisit Say's Law. These "supply-siders" advocated the use of tax cuts, deregulation, and privatization as a method of restoring rapid economic growth. They argued that marginal tax rates were so high that they removed the incentive to work, save, and (most importantly) invest in capital goods to increase the aggregate supply. Excessive government regulation of corporate behavior further dampened the incentive to grow business through investment in capital goods. The Laffer curve (figure 6) demonstrates the relationship between tax rates and government revenue, and counters the argument that higher tax rates generate more tax revenue. Also remember that taxes are viewed as a leakage in AE theory, which diminishes output.

Laffer Curve

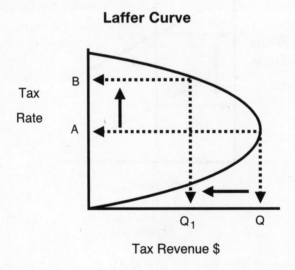

Tax Revenue $

Figure 6

Notice that if the tax rate moves above A to B, tax revenues diminish from Q to Q1. This theory suggests that if tax rates were higher than A, a tax rate cut would not only increase AE total output (aggregate supply), but actually increase government revenues. Critics suggest that tax cuts are not absolute in their positive effect; that they can be inflationary if undertaken when at or near full employment; and that determination of where you are on the Laffer curve is impossible. Finally, tax cuts may result in budget deficits, causing government borrowing, which raises interest rates and crowds out some private investment. (Crowding out is detailed later in relation to fiscal policy.)

FOCUS ON CONSUMER EXPENDITURE

The majority of expenditure in the U.S. economy (around two-thirds) is by household consumers. Consumers may spend or save their disposable (after-tax) income. Therefore, an understanding of consumer behavior is critical to any attempt to effect a change in the state of the overall economy. John Maynard Keynes provided the following analysis. His theory forms the basis of the "Keynesian" view of a general free market economy and dominated U.S. fiscal policy for more than 50 years. A key element of this general theory on economics was that Keynes believed it possible to measure the spending reaction of consumers with a change in disposable income. This is termed the *marginal propensity to consume/save* (MPC/MPS). Consumers have an equilibrium point for their disposable income (DI) relative to their expenditures. Any point of income above this equilibrium will result in a portion of income being saved. Any point below equilibrium will cause consumers to dissave (exhaust money capital or borrow). In conclusion, if government wanted to stimulate spending by consumers, a reduction of taxation would at some point increase spending. Still, not all of the increase in disposable income would be spent. Figure 7 helps us understand this key concept.

Marginal Propensity to Consume or Save

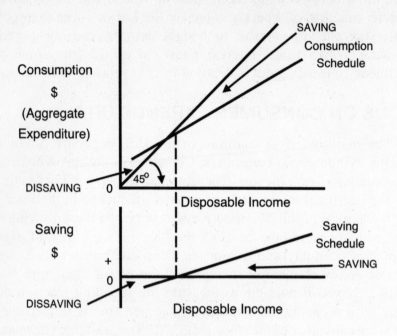

Figure 7

The bisection of the right angle (the 45° line) represents a direct relationship between income and expenditure. In other words, every extra dollar of disposable income received will result in that dollar being expended. The slope of the bisection line is 1. Remember, the formula for the calculation of slope is:

$$\frac{\text{change in vertical}}{\text{change in horizontal}}$$

Therefore, if you determine the slope of actual consumption, you would determine what percentage of income a consumer would spend. The remainder,

$$(1 - MPC) = MPS$$

is the marginal propensity to save. For example, the marginal propensity to consume would be

$$\frac{\text{change in expenditure}}{\text{change in disposable income}} = \frac{15}{20} \text{ or } 0.75 \text{ (slope)}$$

This means that for every $1.00 of increased income over equilibrium, $0.75 would be spent by consumers, and therefore, $0.25 would be saved. For every $1.00 of income lost below equilibrium, $0.25 would be dissaved $(1 - 0.75 = 0.25$ MPS$)$. This formula is applied and shown in figure 8.

Marginal Propensity to Consume or Save

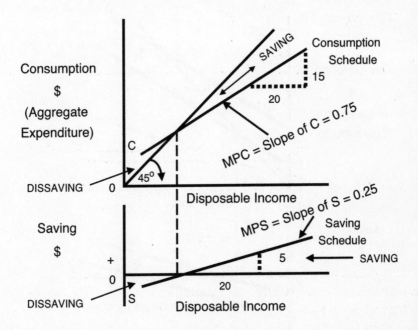

Figure 8

In conclusion, this theory is significant if one wanted to predict the effect that a change in disposable income would have on expenditure. So, if the federal government reduced taxes, DI would increase, increasing expenditure and stimulating expansion of the overall economy. Economic indicators such as the University of Michigan's consumer sentiment index attempt to provide economists with insight into the direction of consumer behavior.

BUSINESS INVESTMENT, INCLUDING GOVERNMENT, AND NET EXPORTS TO THE AE MODEL (INJECTIONS AND LEAKAGES)

Remember that consumer spending (C) is not the only component of AE. Businesses also spend money on investment goods (I_g). Furthermore, government (G) spends money through its annual budgets, and foreign economies spend on our exports. An increase in any of the four components would shift the AE upwards. Just as spending increases cause an upward shift of the AE, leakages (savings, taxes, and imports) of the components would result in a downward shift of AE.

Marginal Propensity to Consume or Save

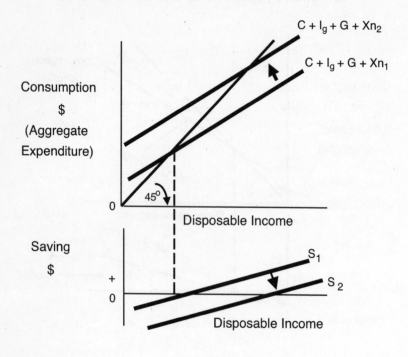

Figure 9

Notice that an increased spending injection in any of the four components of AE results in a movement upward of the entire AE, and a new equilibrium level. Furthermore, since C(MPC) + S(MPS) must equal 1, an upward shift of AE (figure 9) must have an equal shift downward of S, and vice versa. Since all four components may be increasing or decreasing at the same time, a leakage and injection analysis would allow one to predict the net effect of changes in AE on GDP output. This analysis is often expressed algebraically. For example, if consumption (C) increased by $5 billion, business investment (I) remained the same, government spending (G) increased by $5 billion, and imports (M) increased by $5 billion, there would be a net increase in the AE of $5 billion:

$$C + I_g + G + Xn = AE = \$5 + \$0 + \$5 - \$5 = \$5$$

This change in AE would then be subject to the multiplier, and a new equilibrium GDP would result. As seen in figure 10, if the MPS were 0.25 (resulting in a multiplier of 4), then a net injection in AE of $5 billion would result in equilibrium GDP increasing by $20 billion. If the injection described above occurred, and equilibrium GDP was at the $450 billion level, the new equilibrium level would be $470 billion (5 × 4, the multiplier, = 20). What complicates the injection leakage analysis of AE changes (and thus the resulting impact on equilibrium GDP output) is the fact that the leakage of government taxes upon the consumption component are first subject to the MPC/MPS, prior to being subject to the multiplier. This is due to the fact that if a lump sum tax is imposed upon consumers, they would not just reduce their spending, but also their savings. The degree to which they would make this adjustment is determined by the MPC/MPS. This balanced budget gap issue is discussed later, in fiscal policy.

Change in Equilibrium GDP and Investment

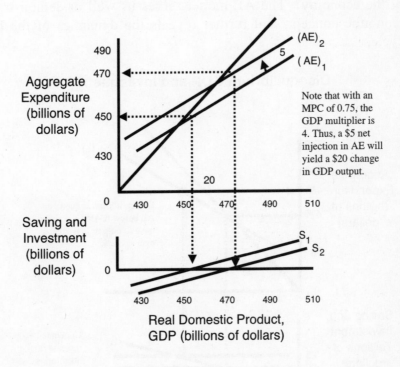

Note that with an MPC of 0.75, the GDP multiplier is 4. Thus, a $5 net injection in AE will yield a $20 change in GDP output.

Real Domestic Product, GDP (billions of dollars)

Figure 10

FOCUS ON I_g AND DISEQUILIBRIUM

A key component of private spending in the AE is gross business investment. This consists of purchased capital goods, inventories, and services that grow the total output (AS) of the economy. The AE model helps to explain how firms react to levels of GDP output greater than and less than equilibrium level (where all production is consumed). In figure 11, we see how firms had planned on an investment of $20 billion ($I_{g_1}$). However, at the $490 GDP output level, consumers spent less and saved more than firms expected (S\$25 > I_g\$20), as seen by the AE (C + I_g)$_1$. The firms had an increase in their inventories, since consumer spending is insufficient at the GDP output of $490 to sell all of the output produced. When this occurs, firms will lay off workers (lessening total income) and reduce their investment in inventories (contraction of the economy) until GDP equilibrium is attained. Conversely, if AE is greater than GDP output (S < I_g), firms will end up with an unplanned decrease in inventory. They will hire workers (increasing total income) and increase output until equilibrium is achieved (expansion of the economy). The AE model serves us well in demonstrating this economic concept, and further reveals the dynamics of the business cycle.

Disequilibrium GDP and Investment

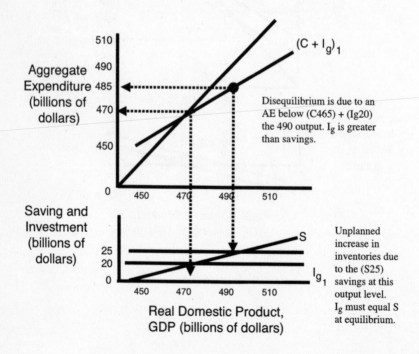

Disequilibrium is due to an AE below (C465) + (Ig20) the 490 output. I_g is greater than savings.

Unplanned increase in inventories due to the (S25) savings at this output level. I_g must equal S at equilibrium.

Real Domestic Product, GDP (billions of dollars)

Figure 11

GDP AND THE MULTIPLIER

Since we now are aware of the effect that changes in the components of AE have on GDP equilibrium, we must explain why a change in AE leads to a larger change in GDP. A concept known as the *multiplier* helps us to determine the exact ratio of change relationship between changes in AE and GDP. The multiplier formula is:

$$\text{Multiplier} = \frac{\text{change in real GDP}}{\text{initial change in spending}}$$

The AE model demonstrates the multiplier graphically (figure 12).

Change in AE and the GDP Multiplier

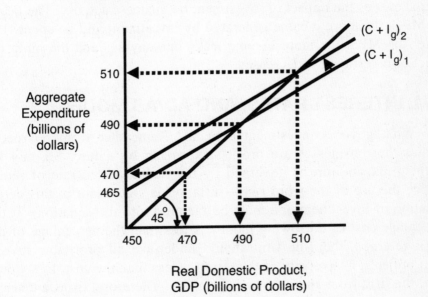

Figure 12

If $(C + I_{g1})$ to $(C + I_{g2})$ represented an increase in I_g of $5 billion ($465 to $470), that increase would result in a change in equilibrium GDP of $20 billion ($490 to $510). If we reversed the shift in $C + I_g$, a $5 billion decrease would cause a $20 billion drop in GDP. How can this initial change in investment spending cause a disproportionate change in AE and GDP? The initial change in spending sets off a spending chain effect in the economy. Remember, the initial investment spending will generate an equal amount of income that is then subject to the MPC and MPS. Furthermore, the initial consumer spending is another household's income, which is also subject to the MPS/ MPC. This cycle repeats itself until the money is exhausted. This money is exhausted when a savings of $5 billion is created, equal to the $5 billion increase in investment spending. There is a relationship between the MPS and the multiplier. If the MPS is 0.25, income would have to increase 4 times more than the savings rate to be equal. So, to save $5 billion, $20 billion of income would have to be available. In other words, the multiplier formula is:

$$\frac{1}{MPS}, \quad so \quad \frac{1}{0.25} = 4 \quad or \quad \frac{1}{1 \pm MPC}, \quad so \quad \frac{1}{1 \pm 0.75} = 4$$

The multiplier helps us to understand why a small change in investment can lead to a larger change in equilibrium GDP. The multiplier shows us the impact of investment on business activity. The larger the MPC, the more income generated by investment will be spent. The larger the MPS, the more income leaks into savings and the more the effect of investment is decreased.

IDM, INTEREST RATES, AND AD/AS MODEL

What governs investment demand? Remember from microeconomics that businesses are profit-maximizing by nature. So, any investment expenditure is governed by the real expected rate of return (notice the use of the word *real*—inflation is significant in this determination of investment and must be factored into the equation). If the percentage cost of borrowing money is less than the percentage of net profit returned, then the firm should undertake all profitable investment projects. Conversely, if the return is less than the cost, loss would repel the firm from any investment venture. Therefore, firms are sensitive to any excessive anticipated inflation or deflation. Moreover, taxation, technological innovation, household debt, consumer sentiment, producer prices, political climate, interest rates, money supply, and stock value also affect a firm's investment expenditure plans. These factors (determinants) cause a shift in a firm's investment demand. The relationship of investment demand (Id) to interest rate (i) and investment quantity is depicted in a very important model (figure 13). Notice the direct relationship between real interest and money invested. Suppose that Congress cut corporate taxes by 20%. What would happen to the Id for money?

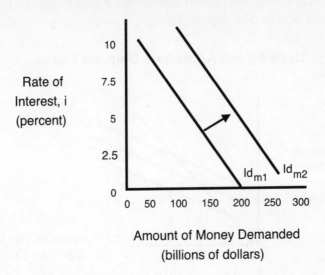

Investment Demand Shifts

Figure 13

The shift in demand for money would cause firms to borrow more money at all interest rates, because their profit would increase by the reduction of tax, making investment more desirable. This relationship between interest rates and investment demand is, as we will see later, a critical component of monetary policy. If you control the money supply, you can affect interest rates and thus encourage or discourage Id, thereby growing or contracting the AE and affecting total output.

AGGREGATE DEMAND/AGGREGATE SUPPLY MODEL

The AD/AS model represents variable price levels relative to changes in output, employment, and income as aggregate demand and aggregate supply equilibrium occurs. The AD curve is determined by the AE equilibrium at various levels of output, as previously described. The AD curve is downward sloping, revealing the effect that inflation/deflation has on spending. The determinants mentioned earlier, viz.:

- change in consumer spending (C)
- change in gross business investment (I_g)
- change in government spending (G)
- change in net export (X_n)

with respect to AE shifts, result in similar shifts of AD. A leftward shift of AD represents decreased spending; a rightward shift indicates increases at all levels. See figure 14.

Deriving the Aggregate Demand Curve

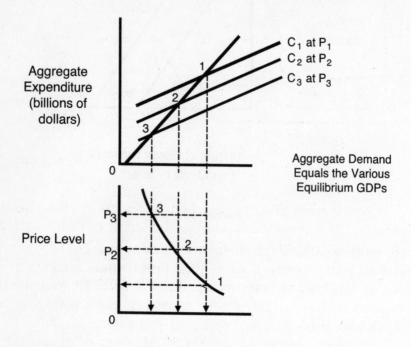

Figure 14

The AS curve represents the various levels of output that businesses will produce at various price levels. Many economists draw the AS curve with three distinct stages: horizontal, transitional, and vertical. Each stage represents a different degree of employment, with horizontal meaning low levels of employment, transitional showing that we are nearing full employment, and vertical signifying full employment (as defined earlier). The transitions from each stage depict the increasing cost of inputs as one nears maximum productivity. Aggregate supply is subject to determinants (such as taxation input costs, expectations, and productivity) that may cause it to shift. A leftward shift of AS_1 to AS_3 would represent increased costs per unit of production. A rightward shift from AS_1 to AS_2 would be a decreased cost per unit of production, due to increased productivity. This is shown in figure 15.

Changes in Aggregate Supply

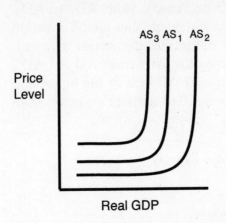

Determinants of Supply
_____

1. Change in input prices
   - Domestic resource availability
     • Land
     • Labor
     • Capital
     • Entrepreneurial ability
   - Prices of imported resources
   - Market power
2. Change in productivity
3. Change in legal institutional environment
   - Business taxes and subsidies
   - Government regulations

Figure 15

The relationship of aggregate demand and aggregate supply reveals the current state of the economy. The model in figure 16 depicts various outcomes of shifts in AD/AS.

The Equilibrium Price Level Real GDP

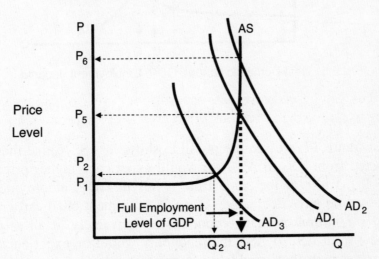

Real Domestic Output, GDP, Employment, Income

Figure 16

Notice that at AD_1/AS equilibrium, there is some rise in price levels, but maximum GDP, employment, and income are achieved. Yet if AD_1 increases to AD_2, the economy cannot produce more g/s to meet that demand. This would result in the rapid increase in price levels that we termed *hyperinflation*. Also, if AD decreased, from AD_1 to AD_3, deflation would result, unemployment would occur, and the GDP would fall. Notice that the model depicts our definition of contraction/recession in the business cycle. If we reversed the AD, from AD_3 to AD_1, we would have an economy in expansion. If AD was in the horizontal stage of AS, there could be an increase in GDP without an increase in the price level.

Shifts in Aggregate Supply

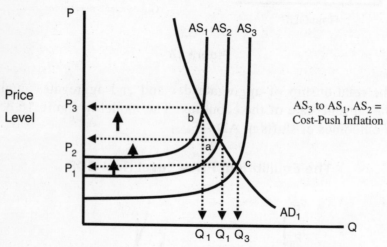

Real Domestic Output, GDP, Employment, Income

Figure 17

In figure 17, we see the possible shifts in AS. Notice that as AS contracted from AS_3 to AS_2, we would experience higher price levels (P_1 to P_2), while at the same time levels of GDP, employment, and income would have decreased (Q_3 to Q_2). As mentioned earlier, this is termed *stagflation* by many economists. Conversely, if an economy's AS grew from AS_1 to AS_3, that economy would be experiencing productivity growth that would lower prices while at the same time increasing GDP, employment, income, and the standard of living. This latter example explains much of our recent prosperity. Also realize that AD and AS can both be moving at the same time, compounding the rate of expansion or contraction. For example, if you had an economy in which AD was increasing while AS was contracting, the rate of inflation would be magnified.

AD/AS AND FISCAL POLICY

The relationship between AD and AS helps us understand demand-pull and cost-push inflation, as well as recessions and expansions in the business cycle. Since the advent of the Keynesians during the Great Depression of the 1930s, the federal government has become increasingly responsible for, and thus involved in, managing our economy's well-being. The U.S. government's fiscal policy has, since the 1930s, worked to create full employment, price stability, and economic growth, with varying degrees of success. What is the rationale behind such behavior, and why do many economists question its effectiveness?

Fiscal policy consists of two basic powers held by the U.S. Congress (subject to approval by the president): taxation and budgetary action spending. Both tend to be structured annually, and may be discretionary (changeable targeted funding) or nondiscretionary (automatic stabilizers) in nature. Policy has two basic directions: expansionary or contractionary. In expansionary fiscal policy, the government is attempting to stimulate the AD by cutting taxes and raising spending levels, or some combination of the two (thereby incurring deficit). In contractionary policy, the government would act to retard the AD through tax increases and spending cuts (thereby incurring surplus). If focused on the consumer, the policy is viewed as (Keynesian) demand-side. If it is focused on business investment, then it is considered (Reaganomics) supply-side.

Equal increases in government taxes and spending result in an increase in GDP output. In other words, if government increased spending by $10 billion and levied a $10 billion lump sum tax, the net effect would be stimulative to the economy by a factor of 1, or $10 billion. Tax cuts/increases are first subject to the MPS/MPC, so tax increases must be larger than spending increases (tax cuts must be larger than spending decreases) to have no effect on the economy's output. This is due to the fact that government spending is subject to the full multiplier, whereas tax cuts are not. To determine the net effect of fiscal policy, one must account for the initial increase or decrease of savings from tax cuts/hikes, then apply the multiplier. For example, if government spends $5 billion (with an MPC of 0.75 the multiplier would be 4), $20 billion would be added to GDP. In order to offset this injection, a lump sum tax with an equal effect must be levied, or the net effect would be a stimulus to the economy. Thus, a $20 billion decrease in GDP through a lump sum tax must be levied. For the tax cut to have a net negative effect on consumption of $5 billion, a tax of $6.67 billion would be required, since 0.25 of the tax payment would come from reduced savings (0.25 × $6.67 billion = $1.67 billion). So by increasing taxes by $6.67 billion—MPS of $1.67 billion = $5 billion—you would offset the spending injection of $5 billion, and there would be no change in the GDP output. If using the MPC to calculate the size of tax necessary to offset government spending, a simple formula can be used: X × MPC = the zero effect tax. Assuming the MPC is 0.80, to offset $20 billion of government spending, one would calculate X × 0.80 = 20, so X = 20/0.80. Thus, X would equal $25 billion. In other words, to offset an injection of $20 billion of government spending, you would have to levy a tax of $25 billion. Remember, at GDP equilibrium, injections equal leakages; Savings + Taxes + M(Imports) = I_g + G + X(Exports).

FISCAL POLICY ISSUES

Some economists advocate government spending as the most direct way to influence the AD. However, what the money gets spent on is a matter of enormous and heated debate. Is government too large and expensive, or are social needs going unmet? Also, the outcome of a tax cut to consumers is unpredictable because it is unclear how much will actually get spent or saved. Tax cuts to business may result only in more profits and not in increased productivity. Serious questions may be raised as to whether tax cuts/increases should be marginal in nature or across the board, by percentage (progressive) or a dollar amount (regressive). Some are concerned that the rich get richer, while others fear that money goes to those who have not earned it. Finally, consider the political implications of an elected official advocating increased taxes and a reduction in government spending programs!

In light of all the issues merely touched on here, it is easy to see why the U.S. government has run annual deficits for decades and accumulated a national debt. Should government accumulate cyclical deficits and pay down debt during years of surplus? How do we finance these deficits? Are politicians capable of recognizing the need for action? Can opposing parties write legislation in time to be effective? How long does it take for laws to be put into action? Many economists have noticed that by the time an expansionary fiscal policy is constructed and put into place, the state of the economy is such that the policy is not only no longer necessary, but may in fact be counterproductive. If it takes 10 months to construct and implement a fiscal policy and a recession lasts 6 months, how effective is the policy?

CROWDING OUT

One of the most fundamental criticisms of fiscal policy concerns the effect that deficit spending has on interest rates. If government funds a deficit by borrowing money, then, by the nature of money markets, the price (interest rate) of money must increase. As the price of money increases (as was noted earlier with regard to AE), investment demand would further weaken, as would interest-sensitive consumer sectors such as housing and automobiles (durable goods). Therefore, any government injection is offset by a reduction in the AE components of $C + I_g$. In terms of the foreign component of AE, if a government seeks money and interest rates increase, foreign capital will be attracted to the United States. This would cause demand for U.S. dollars to increase, and the dollar would appreciate relative to foreign capital. As the dollar appreciated, U.S. goods would become more expensive to the foreign sector and exports would drop. As the dollar appreciated, foreign goods would become cheaper; thus a greater $-X_n$ would further reduce the AE and counteract the U.S. government's expansionary fiscal policy. This can be expressed in terms of the AD/AS model in figure 18.

Expansionary Fiscal Policy and Crowding Out

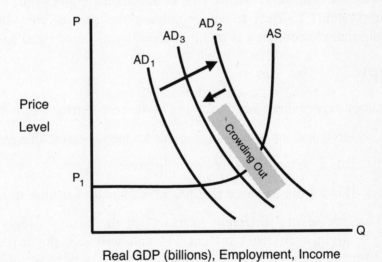

Figure 18

Notice that if the economy were operating in recession at AD_1, and fiscal policy attempted to stimulate the AD_1 to move to AD_2, crowding out would work to counteract the stimulus package and only move the economy to AD_3. Some economists do not believe that the crowding-out effect is that great, as tax cuts may increase profit and stimulate firms to increase investment demand due to greater expectations. Therefore, firms would be willing to borrow money even at the higher interest rates. Also, the Federal Reserve (as we will see in the section on monetarism) could increase the money supply, thereby keeping interest rates from rising, so there would be no crowding out. Finally, some economists observe that tax cuts to consumers tend to effect only a short-run increase in AD that may be inflationary. Demand-siders criticize supply-siders on the bases that the tax-cut incentive to save, invest, and work harder is not very intense, and that tax cuts tend to have long-run effects on growing the AS. These criticisms do not negate the need to consider the economic impact of these variables when constructing fiscal policy.

AD/AS AND MONETARY POLICY

We have already established the importance that money plays in the free market system. A stable money system, and the need for a central bank to manage that system, are accepted as axioms by economists today. In light of the shortcomings of fiscal policy in managing the state of the economy, can we find better management in the Federal Reserve System? Critical to understanding the role of the "Fed" in managing today's economy is an understanding of money and banking.

MONEY

Money serves three key functions in the free market economy:

1. It is a medium of exchange usable for buying and selling g/s.

2. It is a unit of measure defining price.

3. It is a store of value that preserves wealth for later use.

There are several different measures of the money supply, each offering a slightly different insight. As you will see, the investment demand for money relative to the money supply is key to setting interest rates and influencing AE, AD, and the state of the business cycle.

- M_1 = currency and demand deposits

- M_2 = currency, demand deposits, and near money (money market funds, savings accounts, and certificates of deposit of less than \$100,000)

- M_3 = all of the above plus time deposits of more than $100,000

One of the key differences between the different money measurements is the issue of liquidity. *Liquidity* refers to the ease with which an asset can be changed into currency. Stocks and bonds are fairly liquid. Credit cards are not really money, but rather are preapproved loans that are easily accessed. Without question, if you were charged with influencing consumption, the existence of credit cards would complicate your job. Note that the Fed is responsible for maintaining effective control over the money supply; to do so, it focuses on stabilizing the value of money.

Let's revisit the investment demand model (now shown in figure 19) to review the relationship between money supply and investment demand. If the money supply increased from Ms_1 to Ms_2, interest rates (i) would decrease from 7.5% to 2.5% and the quantity of money borrowed for business investment into capital goods would grow ($150 billion to $250 billion). This increase in gross business investment would increase the AE, shift the AD to the right, and should in the long run grow the AS, due to increased productivity, shifting it to the right.

The Money Market

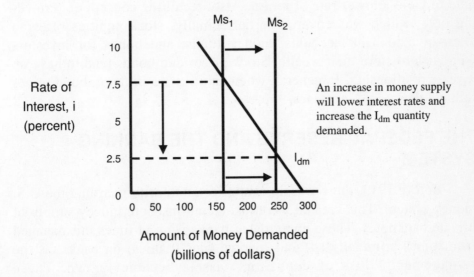

Rate of
Interest, i
(percent)

An increase in money supply will lower interest rates and increase the I_{dm} quantity demanded.

Amount of Money Demanded
(billions of dollars)

Figure 19

BONDS

Bonds play a key role in manipulating the money supply. Money acts as a storehouse of wealth; however, over time any increase in inflation will diminish the value of the stored currency. Furthermore, because others (home buyers through banks, for example) want to borrow your money, they are willing to pay interest to you for its use. Bonds are also a means of storing wealth. In general, a bond is a promissory note, which obligates the borrower to repay the debt's principal and interest at a specific date in the future (the maturity date). Bonds and the money supply tend to have an inverse relationship. When the money supply decreases, the supply of bonds increases, causing bond prices to drop and interest rate yield to increase. For example (using simple rather than compound interest), a $1,000 bond yields $50 of interest at the end of one year. Your interest rate of return would be $50/1,000 = 5\%$. If the supply of bonds increased and the price of the bond fell to $667, then the interest rate would be $50/667$ or 7.5%. (Note that if overall prices are rising, this inflation would deter households from holding currency, which is depreciating in worth). There are many different types of bonds, but for our purposes there are two main kinds: U.S. Government Treasury bonds and corporate bonds. These bonds compete for investors' stored assets. Generally, U.S. Treasuries are viewed as more secure than corporate bonds and thus they tend to yield a lower rate of return. Also, recall the concept of "crowding out," which was covered earlier. Finally, stock equities offer an alternative to bank accounts, money funds, and bonds for investors who wish to store their wealth. Stock prices and bonds tend to have an inverse relationship. In general, when equities are in favor, bond prices fall and their yield increases.

THE FEDERAL RESERVE AND THE BANKING SYSTEM

Before 1913, there was no centralized authority guarding the U.S. money system. This created a confusing and insecure money supply of private banknotes. These unregulated banks were at times mismanaged (sometimes criminally so) and sparked runs (panics) on banks, as the management's loss of depositors' assets became known. These speculatory investments by bankers contributed to severe market expansions and contractions, as evidenced by the Knickerbocker Trust case in 1907. The Panic of 1907, triggered by the losses incurred by copper market speculation of the Knickerbocker Trust president and his associates, provided the necessary impetus for Congress to act. The

Federal Reserve System, established by Congress in 1913, holds power over the money and banking system. Its Board of Governors has 7 members, appointed by the president for staggered 14-year terms. It is the central controlling authority for the system and its power means that the system operates like a central bank. Two sets of bodies assist the Board:

1. The Federal Open Market Committee (FOMC) includes the seven governors plus five regional Federal Reserve Bank presidents, whose terms alternate. They set policy on the buying and selling of government bonds, the most important type of monetary policy.

2. The Federal Advisory Council includes 12 prominent commercial bankers, one from each Fed district, who act as advisors to the Board.

The country is divided into 12 districts, each with its own Federal Reserve Bank and 2 or 3 branch banks. The districts implement the basic directives of the Board of Governors. Each is semi-public, owned by member banks but controlled by the Federal Reserve Board. They act as bankers' banks by accepting reserve deposits and making loans to banks and other financial institutions. The Fed serves many functions, both regulatory and supervisory. Its main purpose is to regulate the supply of money and maintain price stability. The Fed is an independent agency. Its directors, appointed by the president and confirmed by the Senate, have lengthy terms to insulate them from political pressure by elected officials.

TYPES OF BANKS

Commercial banks are privately owned institutions. They consist of state banks (two-thirds of the national total) and national banks (chartered by the federal government). Thrift institutions are regulated by the Treasury Department but are subject to the monetary control of the Fed. They consist of savings and loan associations, mutual savings banks, and credit unions (which are owned by depositors and are run as nonprofit banks). Recent laws have loosened the limitations on the services that banks can offer. The Financial Services Modernization Act of 1999 allows mergers that may well consolidate most financial services, including insurance, within one firm. This consolidation of financial services is taking place globally as well.

BANKS, LOANS, AND THE MONEY MULTIPLIER

One of the three main powers of the Fed is the ability to set the reserve ratio requirement for banks. This power allows a type of banking known as *fractional reserve banking*. This simply means that banks, by law, must put a set percent of their total deposits on reserve with the Fed. For a bank to operate legally, it must maintain a balance between its assets (owned value) and its liabilities (owed value). A simple, typical balance sheet would look like figure 20.

Balance Sheet of a Commercial Bank

ASSETS		=	LIABILITIES	
Cash	$ 0			
Excess Reserve	60,000		Demand Deposits	$ 50,000
Property	240,000		Capital Stock	250,000
Total	$300,000		Total	$300,000

Figure 20

Notice that the assets equal the liabilities. What happens when a $50,000 loan is made to a firm that wants to make a capital-good investment? See the changes to the balance sheet in figure 21.

Balance Sheet of a Commercial Bank

ASSETS		=	LIABILITIES	
Cash	$ 0			
Excess Reserve	60,000		Demand Deposits	$100,000
Loans	50,000		Capital Stock	250,000
Property	240,000		Total	$350,000
Total	$350,000			

Figure 21

"New money" in the amount of $50,000 was created. When a bank makes a loan, it creates money. A bank may create as much money as its excess reserves allow. When a loan is created, the money supply increases; when a loan is repaid, the money supply constricts. When the firm repays the loan, the money is destroyed. If the Fed decreases the reserve ratio, more money can be loaned (easy money). If the reserve ratio is increased, less money can be loaned (tight money). Money is borrowed from a bank with the intention of spending it, on g/ s by the consumer or on investment goods by firms. What they are spending is another person's income. When people receive income, they deposit that money into a bank, which in turn loans it to another household or firm. This process is the core of the money multiplier. Like the MPS concept, the monetary multiplier is the inverse of the required reserve (1/required reserve ratio). So, if the reserve ratio requirement (a bank's MPS, if you will) is 20%, what is the multiplier? Solution: $1/0.20 = 5$.

If $1,000 is deposited into a bank, $5,000 will be added to the money supply before the deposit-loan-redeposit-reloan cycle runs its course. The money supply, therefore, depends heavily on banks' willingness to loan money. Bankers are subject to determinants of supply, so they may during expansion be overly liberal in loaning and during contraction extremely conservative. Banks thus tend to intensify the business cycle. The Fed plays a key role in countering this tendency, which is why you often hear the Fed referred to as a countercyclical institution. This simply means that when recession occurs, the Fed acts in a way that encourages banks to increase lending, thereby stimulating the economy out of contraction. If the business cycle is overexpanding, the Fed acts to discourage loans, thereby going against the cycle. Why put so much effort into regulating the economy? Simply stated, people prefer an economy that avoids the human suffering present during a recession. The Federal Reserve is charged with the mission to achieve and maintain price stability, full employment, and sustainable economic growth through monetary policy.

THE FED AND MONETARY POLICY

The Fed operates much like the banks mentioned earlier. It too must maintain a balance sheet that is solvent, with assets that equal or exceed liabilities. The Fed's balance sheet consists of loans to commercial banks, reserves of commercial banks, cash (Federal Reserve Notes) reserves, Treasury deposits, and Treasury Bills (government bonds). The purchase and sale of this last item (open market operations) is the main source of monetary policy power. It is the Fed's main policy tool to influence the money supply. This ability to operate in the bond market was confirmed in the Accord of 1951 negotiated between the U.S. Treasury and the most powerful arm of the Federal Reserve System, the Federal Open Market Committee (FOMC). As noted earlier, this group consists of the seven members of the Board of

Governors and five regional bank presidents, four of whom rotate on a two-year term (the New York Federal Reserve Bank president is a permanent voting member). Each member has one vote to determine board policy. All bank presidents participate in private discussions, which are published on a delayed basis. Some economists argue that this panel holds the health of the U.S. economy in their hands and thus should be more open to the public. Some even go so far as to say that the FOMC should be replaced by a fixed set of rules that would force them to act in a set way to changes in economic indicators. Most economists counter that the Fed has been very successful in regulating the economy, and point out that tying it to fixed responses may jeopardize our economic well-being.

FOMC

The FOMC meets approximately every six weeks to analyze economic indicators (they publish a "beige book" full of them), gauge the state of the economy, and conclude a "recession watch, neutral, or inflation watch." They announce the federal funds target rate (the rate for overnight borrowing from other banks' reserves), the discount rate (the rate at which banks borrow from the Fed's funds), and direct the New York Federal Reserve Bank to buy/sell government bonds from/to commercial banks and the general public (see the previous section on bonds). This is the most important instrument for influencing the money supply, interest rates, and investment demand. These acts stimulate or constrain the AD, thus influencing prices, GDP, employment, and disposable income.

If inflation is the problem, the Fed sells government bonds to remove money from the economy. This raises interest rates, leading to less investment spending, which in turn lowers AD. Household consumption (C) is indirectly affected as the federal funds rate influences consumer credit rates. Because consumer credit rates are higher than the prime interest rate at which firms borrow, consumer borrowing and spending are negatively impacted. This tightening of the money supply is depicted in figure 22.

The Money Market and FOMC Sale of Bonds

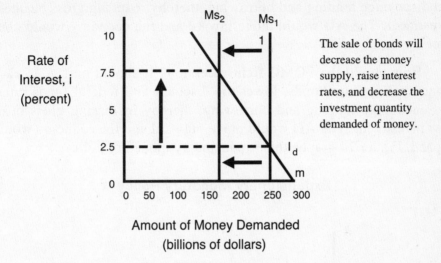

Figure 22

This decrease in money reduces the gross business investment component of AE and shifts the AD to the left. Notice the decreased GDP output, employment, and disposable income in the economy shown in figure 23. The decrease in price levels is greatest if the economy is in stage 2 or 3 inflation.

Contractory Monetary Policy

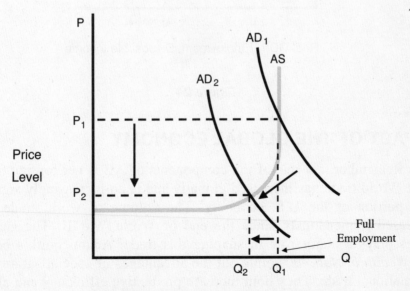

Real GDP, Employment, Disposable Income

Figure 23

How would the FOMC fight inflation? It should pursue a tight money policy: sell bonds, raise the discount and federal funds rates, and discourage lending and borrowing, thereby reducing gross business investment. The AD would move inward and the economy would contract.

How would the FOMC fight recession? It should pursue an easy money policy: buy bonds, lower the discount and federal funds rates, and encourage lending and borrowing, thereby increasing gross business investment. The AD would move outward and the economy would expand. Figure 24 graphs this expansionary monetary policy.

Expansionary Monetary Policy

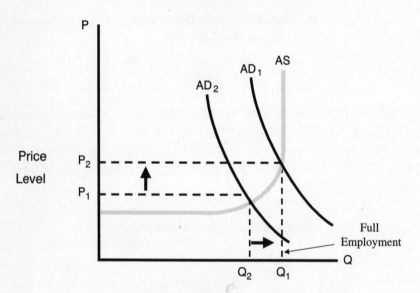

Real GDP, Employment, Disposable Income

Figure 24

IMPACT OF THE GLOBAL ECONOMY

Remember that one of the components of AE is net foreign trade (X_n). World trade has increased globally and is an increasingly significant portion of the U.S. economy. The volume of world trade has increased tremendously since the end of World War II. The United States plays a major role in shaping this trade. Adam Smith's book, *The Wealth of Nations*, points out the advantages of specialization and international trade. They both increase productive efficiency and allow greater total output than would otherwise be possible. Production possibilities tables allow us to quantify the efficiency gains of specialization. This is known as the *principle of comparative advantage*.

NAFTA AND GATT

Three major international agreements have furthered the movement toward a global economy: the 1958 EU, the 1993 NAFTA, and the 1995 Uruguay GATT. The European Union ("common market") comprises 15 European nations. The EU has formed a powerful trade bloc, reducing or eliminating tariffs among its members while at the same time establishing tariffs on g/s from outside. Some U.S. firms have argued that this bloc makes it difficult for them to compete within the EU. One of the most recent, controversial, and significant accomplishments of the EU was the establishment of a common currency, the *euro*.

Somewhat in response to the growing power of the EU, was the 1993 North American Free Trade Agreement, forming a major trade bloc of Canada, Mexico, and the United States. This trade agreement, which is to be phased in by 2008, established a free-trade zone designed to reduce and eventually eliminate tariffs and other trade barriers among the signatories. Recently, Latin American nations have expressed an interest in expanding the benefits of NAFTA to all of Central and South America.

The 1995 General Agreement on Tariffs and Trade (GATT) established the World Trade Organization (WTO) as a permanent successor to the less formal GATT negotiations. China's recent entrance into the WTO has broadened the reach of the organization to more than 140 nations. Although in some ways incomplete, the WTO provides for some standardization on significant trade issues such as protectionist quotas, subsidies, and trademark, patent, or copyright infringement. Structural resolution of trade disputes is possible in WTO institutions, with approved tariff punishment for violators.

Both the NAFTA and the GATT have proponents as well as critics. Critics are concerned that firms will be able to circumvent U.S. laws that protect workers and the environment. Are labor unions, worker safety laws, minimum wage laws, and environmental protection rules effective if firms can shift production to nations that are weak in these areas? Proponents counter that most of the world's trade is among advanced industrial nations that have well-established worker and environmental protection laws. Adherents argue that as the free flow of g/s raises the output and disposable income levels in poorer nations, the increase in living standards will engender stronger laws, thereby spreading free market benefits across the world.

The new rules have created intense competition between firms. The tendency of firms to survive competition through merger and acquisition has hastened the formation of new multinational companies. These multinationals, as the name implies, produce and distribute g/s globally.

COMPARATIVE ADVANTAGE

The principle of comparative advantage is based on the law of increasing opportunity costs. Opportunity costs reflect the differing levels of inputs and technology present within a country. When two nations are compared as to efficiency of production of certain goods, we can see which total output is the greatest, resulting in the lowest cost. Even though one nation may enjoy absolute advantage over another in the production of goods, it serves both nations' best interests to seek the lower domestic opportunity cost for the less productive nation. This is made clear in the following table of production possibilities (table 1).

Table 1

Canada's production possibilities table (millions of gallons)

Product	Production alternatives			
	A	B	C	D
Apple juice	0	20	40	60
Maple syrup	60	40	20	0
	Total 60			

United States production possibilities table (millions of gallons)

Product	Production alternatives			
	E	F	G	H
Apple juice	0	10	20	30
Maple syrup	15	10	5	0
	Total 20			

In this example, notice that Canada has greater total productivity in both apple juice (60) and maple syrup (60) when compared to U.S. apple juice (30) and maple syrup (15). Canada has a cost advantage over the United States in both products. Now what? Should the United States give up all production? Should it make only apple juice, only maple syrup, or some combination? Comparative advantage tells us that the United States should produce its lower domestic opportunity cost product, apple juice. We know this because it must sacrifice 10 units of apple juice to get 5 units of syrup, so 1 unit of apple juice is 0.5 units of syrup. The cost to Canada is greater, as it must give up 1 unit of maple syrup to gain 1 unit of apple juice. The United States should produce apple juice while Canada produces maple syrup. The result is more total apple juice and syrup produced. Canada will produce 60 units of maple syrup and the United States will produce 30 units of apple juice, for a total of 90 units produced. If Canada produced at the B level while the United States produced at the F level, a total of 80 units of goods would be produced. There is a net gain of 10 units of extra produce to be divided between the countries. Both end up with more juice and syrup! The trade exchange rate would end up with Canada wanting 1 unit of syrup for > 1 units of U.S. apple juice. The United States would want to get > 0.5 units of syrup for 1 unit of juice. The actual exchange would be determined by other factors, such as total world demand and supply. If the exchange rate ended up at 1 unit of syrup for 1.6 units of juice, then Canada could keep 45 units of maple syrup (gain of 5; see B column) and trade for 24 (gain of 4) units of apple juice. The United States would keep 6 (gain of 6) units of apple juice and get 15 (same as before at maximum production) units of maple syrup. Notice that both nations have more than if they pursued independent production.

FINANCING INTERNATIONAL TRADE

A major stumbling block to trade between nations is the involvement of different national currencies. An American firm exporting a g/s to a Brazilian does not want to be paid in Brazilian riales, because that currency cannot be spent in the United States. So, the importer must exchange its currency for U.S. dollars. This service is provided (for a fee) by major banks that have created currency exchanges.

U.S. exports cause an increased demand by Brazilians for U.S. dollars. The increased foreign demand for the U.S. dollar increases the supply of the foreign currency in exchange markets. U.S. imports would increase the demand for the foreign currency and would increase the supply of U.S. dollars in exchange markets. This situation is graphically portrayed in figure 25. Notice that as the demand for U.S. dollars increased from D to D_1, the number of riales needed to purchase that dollar increased from 5 to 7.5.

The Currency Money Market

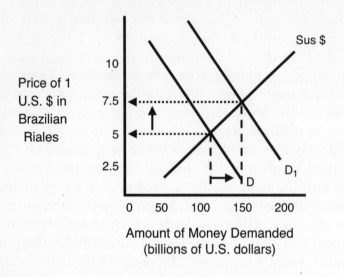

Figure 25

BALANCE OF PAYMENTS

Balance of payments refers to the sum of all currency transactions covering imports and exports. If a nation imports more than it exports, it has an unfavorable balance of trade. If a nation exports more than it imports, it has a favorable balance of trade. The implications of trade deficits or surpluses can get complicated. Economists divide a nation's balance of trade into three accounts: current, capital, and official reserves. The current account is exports – imports + net investment income (net interest and dividends paid by foreigners to Americans) + net transfers (foreign aid, money sent to Americans or their families living overseas). The capital account sums the balance of purchases and sales of real assets (real estate, office buildings) and financial assets (common stock, corporate bonds). The official reserves account consists of the foreign currencies held by a nation's central bank. These reserves are increased or decreased in reaction to the balance of the current and capital accounts. If the balance is negative, a deficit is noted; if it is positive, a benefit is noted. Whether a deficit or surplus is good or bad depends on how the issue is resolved.

CURRENCY EXCHANGE RATES

There are two major types of currency exchange formats: floating and fixed. At the end of World War II, 44 nations met and created the Bretton Woods system. The U.S. dollar served as the focal point of this system because the U.S. dollar became the reserve currency of the system. Countries bought and sold dollars to maintain their exchange rates. The value of the U.S. dollar was fixed at $35 per ounce of gold and was convertible on demand for foreigners holding U.S. dollars. The dollar became as good as gold.

Two new organizations were also created at the Bretton Woods Conference, the International Monetary Fund and the World Bank. The IMF was created to supervise the exchange-rate practices of member nations. It also was intended to lend money to nations that were unable to meet their payment obligations (that is, to do "bailouts"). IMF funds come from fees charged to the 178 member nations. The World Bank, funded through the sale of bonds, loans money to developing nations for economic development. The Bretton Woods system dissolved in 1971 as the U.S. dollar came under devaluation pressure and gold drained from the nation's reserves. In March 1973, a managed, floating exchange rate was established by the major industrial countries. Central banks of various nations have at times intervened to alter their nation's currency value. An example of this occurred in 1995 when the Fed and U.S. Treasury bought German marks and Japanese yen to increase the value of the dollar, which they thought had fallen excessively. The managed float has withstood severe economic upheaval, such as the OPEC oil crisis in 1973. Some nations, to maintain a more stable domestic currency, have "pegged" the value of their currency to a fixed rate with the U.S. dollar or another industrial nation's currency. An independent floating exchange rate would be subject to the laws of supply and demand in the currency marketplace.

For example, assume that the nation of Argentina imported more g/s from the United States than it exported. The market for the Argentine peso would look like the model in figure 26. Notice that as the demand for the U.S. dollar increases, to pay for the imports, the price of the U.S. dollar relative to the Argentine peso increases. In other words, the value of the Argentine peso depreciates while the U.S. dollar appreciates, as seen in figure 26.

The Currency Money Market

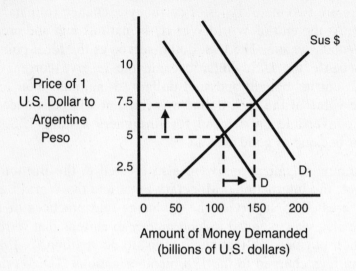

Figure 26

This has significant trade implications. Because of poor management of their government's fiscal/monetary policy, some nations may have to endure a major depreciation of their currency. The impact of depreciation in our example would be a significant reduction in Argentina's ability to import American g/s. At the same time, the cheaper Argentine peso would make its goods cheaper to Americans and should stimulate U.S. demand for Argentine g/s. The impact of currency appreciation/depreciation gives us the main impetus for long-run trade equilibrium. For less industrialized nations that depend on export of farm products and raw materials, currency fluctuations may lead to serious destabilization of the domestic economy. The lack of price stability and increased unemployment resulting from economic contraction in the cycle may result in political upheaval. Over the past several years, the United States has recorded large trade deficits, primarily with Japan and China. At the same time, the U.S. rate of savings has declined to finance increased imports. Many of these dollars have returned to the United States in the form of greater foreign asset ownership. Those concerned about this trade deficit point to the jobs lost to overseas producers and the loss of U.S. assets to foreign ownership. Others point to the increased standard of living achieved and assert that the foreign assets invested in the United States increase our production capacity, which will create the output necessary to service the foreign debt in the long run. The long-term outcome of this situation is unknown.

MACROECONOMICS TEST

AP Macroeconomics

TEST

Section I

TIME: 70 minutes
       60 multiple-choice questions

(Answer sheets appear in the back of this book.)

DIRECTIONS: Each of the questions or incomplete statements below is followed by five suggested answers or completions. Select the best for each question and then fill in the corresponding oval on the answer sheet.

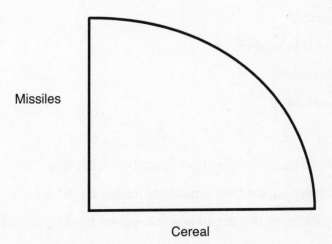

Missiles

Cereal

1. Which of the following would cause the production possibilities curve shown above to shift outward?

   (A) Reopening a cereal plant that had been closed

   (B) Rehiring laid-off cereal workers

   (C) Using machinery for missile production instead of cereal production

(D)   Using machinery for cereal production instead of missile production

(E)   Developing a more efficient cereal-making process

2.   Which of the following is an example of an economic trade-off?

(A)   A 12% rate of return on an investment

(B)   Reducing unemployment while increasing economic growth

(C)   Increasing the national savings rate while investment spending rises

(D)   Spending less on education programs due to an increase in military spending

(E)   Buying milk and cookies

3.   Because resources are _____, trade-offs between alternative uses of those resources must be made.

(A)   available

(B)   scarce

(C)   sold in markets

(D)   tangible

(E)   unlimited

4.   Which of the following best describes "efficiency"?

(A)   Spending the least amount of money for an item

(B)   Obtaining the largest possible output from limited resources

(C)   Production of the items that are most in demand

(D)   An equal distribution of scarce resources

(E)   Lowering the price on your goods so that you sell more goods

5. Suppose two countries are each capable of individually producing two given products. Instead, each specializes by producing the good for which it has a comparative advantage and then trades with the other country. Which of the following is most likely to result?

   (A) Both countries will benefit from increased production of goods.

   (B) Unemployment will increase in one country and decrease in the other.

   (C) There will be more efficient production in one country but less efficient production in the other.

   (D) The two countries will become more independent of each other.

   (E) Both countries will be harmed by increased productive inefficiency.

6. Another way to define GDP is as the market value of

   (A) the resource inputs used in the production of output in an economy.

   (B) all final goods and services produced in an economy in a given year.

   (C) all final and intermediate goods and services produced in a given year.

   (D) national income earned by consumers, producers, and exporters.

   (E) national income earned by producers and consumers.

7. The economic indicator that measures the price change over time, using a fixed market basket of typical goods and services, is the

   (A) producer price index.

   (B) consumer sentiment index.

   (C) GDP.

    (D) CPI.

    (E) national income index.

8.   From an economist's perspective, which of the following is not considered to be investment (I_g)?

    (A) Purchasing new computers for the accounting office

    (B) Building a new plant facility

    (C) Buying back outstanding shares of company stock

    (D) Building an office complex

    (E) Increases in the warehouse inventories of finished product

9.   The expenditures or output approach to measuring GDP does so by totaling

    (A) spending by employees and businesses on rent, resource inputs, and consumption of fixed capital.

    (B) payments to employees, rents, interest, dividends, undistributed corporate profits, proprietors' income, indirect business taxes paid, consumption of fixed capital, and net foreign factor income earned in the United States.

    (C) payments to employees, rents, interest, dividends, corporate profits, proprietors' income, and indirect business taxes, and subtracting the consumption of fixed capital.

    (D) spending for consumption, investment, net exports, and government purchases.

    (E) the total spending for consumption and government purchases, but subtracting public and private transfer payments.

10.   During the expansion phase of the business cycle

    (A) the inflation rate decreases, but productive capacity increases.

    (B) the inflation rate and productive capacity decrease.

    (C) employment, income, and output decrease.

(D) employment increases, but output decreases.

(E) employment, income, and output increase.

11. A headline reads: "Auto sales decline and the steel industry suffers a slump; unemployment rises." This type of unemployment can best be characterized in economic terms as

(A) frictional.

(B) structural.

(C) total unemployment.

(D) cyclical.

(E) natural.

12. Kevin has lost his job in an automobile plant because the company began using robots for welding on the assembly line. Kevin plans to go to technical school to learn how to repair microcomputers. The type of unemployment Kevin is faced with is

(A) frictional.

(B) structural.

(C) educational.

(D) cyclical.

(E) natural.

13. At the full employment unemployment rate, there is/are only

(A) cyclical and frictional unemployment.

(B) downward pressure on wage rates.

(C) frictional and structural unemployment.

(D) cyclical unemployment.

(E) undercounted "discouraged workers" unemployment.

AD/AS

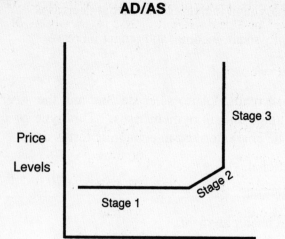

Output, Income, and Employment

14. Refer to the preceding diagram. A decrease in total spending in Stage 2 will

    (A) decrease the price level, but not employment and output.

    (B) decrease employment and output, but not the price level.

    (C) decrease employment, output, and the price level.

    (D) increase employment, output, and the price level.

    (E) cause unemployment and inflation.

15. Refer to the preceding diagram. An increase in total spending in Stage 3 will increase

    (A) output and decrease price levels.

    (B) employment and the price level.

    (C) output and the price level.

    (D) the price level, but not output or employment.

    (E) the price level and decrease the natural rate of unemployment.

16. An increase in transportation costs will most likely cause the price level and real GDP to change in which of the following ways?

	Price Level	Real GDP
(A)	increase	increase
(B)	increase	decrease
(C)	increase	no change
(D)	decrease	increase
(E)	decrease	decrease

17. Select the statement most associated with Classical economists that Keynes disagreed with.

   (A) A market economy eventually results in monopolies that damage the standard of living.

   (B) Market economies function best when government makes supply decisions.

   (C) Market economies are generally free from price and output cycles.

   (D) A market economy is self-correcting and thus will eventually recover from recession without intervention.

   (E) The factor market underpays workers without minimum wage laws.

18. Based on the circular flow model,

   (A) government plays no role in the flow of goods and services.

   (B) households are suppliers in the product market and consumers are suppliers in the factor market.

   (C) firms purchase goods in the product market.

   (D) households expend their income in the product market and earn their income in the factor market.

   (E) firms incur costs in the product market and obtain revenue in the factor market.

19. In the aggregate expenditures model, the primary determinant of the level of consumption and saving in the economy is the

    (A) inflation rate.

    (B) level of investment.

    (C) level of income.

    (D) level of prices.

    (E) interest rate.

20. Consumers purchase bonds, rather than continuing to hold currency, because they believe that interest rates will decline in the future. Such purchases point to which of the following scenarios?

    (A) There has been an upward shift in consumers' marginal propensity to consume.

    (B) Consumers expect little need for cash.

    (C) Consumers expect the value of currency to appreciate in the short term.

    (D) Consumers speculate that currency will depreciate in the future.

    (E) Bonds will drop in value relative to currency.

21. In a closed private economy, if the interest rate falls, businesses expect expansion of the economy, and as a result the investment demand also rises, then the

    (A) expenditure equilibrium will shift downward and GDP will decline.

    (B) investment schedule and aggregate expenditures schedule will shift upward.

    (C) investment and aggregate expenditures schedules will shift downward with greater unemployment.

    (D) investment schedule will shift upward and the aggregate expenditures schedule will shift downward, and output will decrease.

    (E) investment schedule will shift downward and the aggregate expenditures schedule will shift upward.

22. In a closed economy with no government, an increase in autonomous investment of $25 billion increases domestic output from $600 billion to $700 billion. The marginal propensity to consume is

    (A) 0.25 and the multiplier is 4.

    (B) 0.50 and the multiplier is 2.

    (C) 0.75 and the multiplier is 4.

    (D) 0.80 and the multiplier is 5.

    (E) the MPS is 0.75 with a multiplier of 4.

23. Other things being equal, if U.S. steel exports fell, the economy would see a(n)

    (A) increase in domestic aggregate expenditures and the equilibrium level of GDP.

    (B) decrease in domestic aggregate expenditures and the equilibrium level of GDP.

    (C) decrease in government spending and a decrease in GDP.

    (D) zero effect on domestic GDP, because imports will offset the change in exports.

    (E) decrease in the marginal propensity to balance trade.

24. Leakages from the income-expenditure stream are

    (A) consumption, saving, and transfers.

    (B) investment, spending, and transfer payments.

    (C) saving, taxes, and transfers.

    (D) saving, taxes, and imports.

    (E) imports, taxes, and transfers.

25. If a lump-sum tax of $40 billion is levied and the MPS is 0.25, then the saving schedule will shift

    (A) upward by $10 billion.

    (B) downward by $160 billion.

    (C) upward by $25 billion.

    (D) downward by $10 billion.

    (E) downward by $25 billion.

26. If a government raises its expenditure by $25 billion and at the same time levies a lump-sum tax of $25 billion, the net effect on the economy will be to

    (A) increase GDP by $25 billion.

    (B) increase GDP by less than $100 billion, because the multiplier is 4.

    (C) increase GDP by more than $50 billion.

    (D) increase GDP by $50 billion.

    (E) make no change in GDP.

Aggregate Expenditure

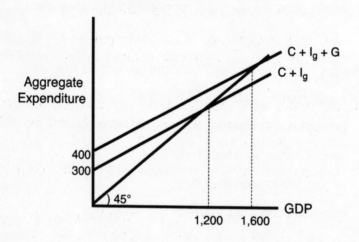

27. Refer to the preceding graph. The size of the multiplier associated with changes in government spending in this economy is

    (A) 2.50.

    (B) 3.00.

    (C) 5.00.

    (D) 6.67.

    (E) 4.00.

28. Refer to the preceding graph. If this economy is a closed economy without a government sector, the level of GDP would be

    (A) $1,200 billion.

    (B) $200 billion.

    (C) $300 billion.

    (D) $1,600 billion.

    (E) $500 billion.

29. As Americans increase their purchase of foreign goods and services, the aggregate expenditure relationship to the aggregate demand and supply model would indicate that a

    (A) fall in our aggregate expenditure will cause domestic price level to decrease, aggregate demand to fall, and GDP to decline.

    (B) fall in our domestic price level will decrease our imports and increase our exports, thereby reducing the net exports component of aggregate demand.

    (C) fall in our domestic price levels will decrease our imports and reduce unemployment.

    (D) rise in our domestic price level will increase our imports and reduce our exports, thereby reducing the net exports component of aggregate demand.

(E) rise in our domestic price level will decrease our imports and increase our exports, thereby reducing the net exports component of aggregate demand.

30. Which combination of factors would most likely increase aggregate demand?

(A) A decrease in consumer debt and an increase in the value of the dollar

(B) An increase in consumer debt and a decrease in foreign demand for products

(C) An increase in the money supply and a decrease in interest rates

(D) An increase in personal taxes and a decrease in government spending

(E) An increase in business taxes and a decrease in corporate earnings

31. If the economy is operating in stage 2, the intermediate range, of aggregate supply, and business investment decreases, then price level, income, and employment would most likely change in which of the following ways?

	Price Level	Income	Employment
(A)	increase	increase	increase
(B)	increase	increase	decrease
(C)	increase	decrease	increase
(D)	decrease	increase	decrease
(E)	decrease	decrease	decrease

32. Which would most likely shift aggregate supply to the right?

    (A) An increase in corporate income tax

    (B) A decrease in the value of the dollar and an increase in the prices of imported products

    (C) An increase in minimum wage

    (D) A decrease in business subsidies

    (E) Improvements in technology

33. If firms experienced a large and rapid unplanned decrease in inventories, we would anticipate

    (A) a reduction in workforce.

    (B) a decrease in imports.

    (C) an increase in inflation.

    (D) a decline in income.

    (E) a decrease in price levels.

34. In the short run, an expansionary fiscal policy will cause aggregate demand, employment, and price level to react in which of the following combinations?

	Aggregate Demand	Employment	Price Level
(A)	decrease	decrease	decrease
(B)	increase	increase	increase
(C)	no change	no change	decrease
(D)	increase	decrease	increase
(E)	decrease	increase	no change

35. If aggregate demand increases and, as a result, the price level increases, while real domestic output and employment are unaffected, we can assume that

    (A) aggregate demand intersects aggregate supply in the intermediate range of the aggregate supply curve.

    (B) aggregate demand intersects aggregate supply in the vertical range of the aggregate supply curve.

    (C) aggregate demand intersects aggregate supply in the horizontal range of the aggregate supply curve.

    (D) aggregate supply increases to accommodate the change in aggregate demand.

    (E) aggregate supply has shifted inward due to foreign supply shock.

36. The economy experiences an increase in the price level, a decrease in real domestic output, and increased unemployment. Which of the following is the most likely cause?

    (A) Increased productivity

    (B) Increased input prices

    (C) Decreased excess capacity

    (D) Reduced government regulations

    (E) Increased exports

37. Which of the following would a Keynesian recommend to combat high inflation?

    (A) No change in taxation and increased subsidy

    (B) Increased taxation and increased government spending

    (C) Increased taxation and decreased government spending

    (D) Decreased taxation and no change in government spending

    (E) No change in taxation and increased government spending

38. An economy is experiencing hyperinflation. The government wants to reduce household consumption by $48 billion to reduce inflationary pressure. The MPC is 0.75. Which of the following government actions would achieve its objective?

    (A) Increasing spending by $48 billion

    (B) Raising taxes by $6 billion

    (C) Increasing spending by $9 billion and raising taxes by $48 billion

    (D) Raising taxes by $12 billion

    (E) Raising taxes by $16 billion

39. Automatic stabilizers reduce the severity of business cycle fluctuations because they produce changes in the government's budget that

    (A) result in long-run balanced budgets.

    (B) result in constant growth of GDP.

    (C) help offset changes in employment.

    (D) produce a cyclically adjusted budget.

    (E) produce a full employment budget.

40. One of the criticisms of fiscal policy as a means of regulating the state of the economy is that an "operational lag" occurs between the

    (A) beginning of a recession or inflationary period and the time that it takes for government to become aware of it.

    (B) levying of a tax and collection of the revenue.

    (C) time the need for fiscal action is recognized and the time that legislation is passed.

    (D) time that fiscal action is taken and the time that action has an impact on output, employment, and the price level.

    (E) time that taxes have an impact on output, employment, and the price level and the time by which it can be determined if the tax policy is effective.

41. The crowding-out effect suggests that

    (A) an increase in household consumption is always at the expense of saving.

    (B) any increase in MPC effects a reduction in MPS.

    (C) government budget spending increases close a recessionary gap.

    (D) government deficit spending may raise the interest rate and thereby reduce investment.

    (E) government borrowing increases the money supply and encourages business investment, thereby reducing household borrowing.

42. The United States is experiencing inflation, so Congress adopts a contractionary fiscal policy to reduce inflation. The net export effect suggests that net exports would

    (A) decrease due to the resulting decrease in interest rates, thus decreasing aggregate demand and partially reinforcing the fiscal policy.

    (B) increase, as the decline in the value of the dollar would increase exports.

    (C) decrease, thus increasing aggregate demand and partially offsetting the fiscal policy.

    (D) increase, thus decreasing aggregate demand and partially reinforcing the fiscal policy.

    (E) increase as imports decreased, thus increasing aggregate demand and partially offsetting the fiscal policy.

43. A senator calls for legislation reducing corporate taxes, to increase investment and promote economic growth. This senator would most likely be advocating a

    (A) contractionary fiscal policy.

    (B) reduction in automatic stabilizers.

    (C) nondiscretionary fiscal policy.

(D) supply-side fiscal policy.

(E) growth in aggregate demand through fiscal policy.

44. Other things being equal, the international value of foreign currencies will decrease against the U.S. dollar ($) if

(A) U.S. citizens increase spending on foreign goods.

(B) U.S. businesses reduce exports.

(C) the U.S. Federal Reserve lowers real interest rates.

(D) the number of foreign tourists to Disney World decreases.

(E) foreigners increase deposits into U.S. money markets.

International Trade

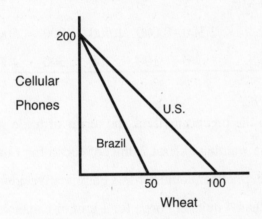

45. The domestic opportunity cost of producing 200 cellular phones in the U.S. is 100 bushels of wheat. In Brazil, the domestic opportunity cost of producing 200 cellular phones is 50 bushels of wheat. In this case,

(A) Brazil has a comparative advantage in the production of wheat.

(B) 1 cellular phone costs the United States only 0.25 bushels of wheat.

(C) the United States has a comparative advantage in the production of cellular phones.

(D) mutual gains from trade can be obtained if the United States imports cellular phones from Brazil and Brazil imports wheat from the United States.

(E) mutual gains from trade can be obtained if the United States imports wheat from Brazil and Brazil imports televisions from the United States.

Nigeria's Production Possibilities

Commodity Mix	A	B	C	D	E	F
Cocoa	750	600	450	300	150	0
Banana	0	50	100	150	200	250

Colombia's Production Possibilities

Commodity Mix	A	B	C	D	E	F
Cocoa	2,500	2,000	1,500	1,000	500	0
Banana	0	100	200	300	400	500

46. Based upon the preceding data, the terms of trade will be

(A) Nigeria wanting at least 2 units of cocoa for 1 unit of banana.

(B) no trade; neither country has a comparative advantage.

(C) more than 4 units of cocoa for 1 unit of banana.

(D) Nigeria wanting more than 5 units of banana for 1 unit of cocoa and Colombia wanting more than 3 units of banana for 1 unit of cocoa.

(E) Nigeria wanting more than 3 units of cocoa for 1 unit of banana and Colombia wanting more than 1 unit of banana for every 5 units of cocoa.

47. The U.S. FTC finds Japan guilty of "dumping" steel in the U.S. market. Select the description of a protective tariff response.

(A) The United States places an excise tax on products that are not produced domestically in order to raise revenues for the steel industry.

(B) The United States places an excise tax on Japanese steel producers, putting them at a competitive disadvantage in selling steel in U.S. domestic markets.

(C) The United States sets a specific maximum amount of steel that may be imported, in a given period of time, to protect U.S. producers of steel.

(D) U.S. steel firms would no longer be allowed to export steel products to Japan.

(E) The United States restricts the issuance of licenses for imported products and sets unreasonable standards for quality or safety in order to restrict imports of steel and protect domestic markets.

48. An inflow of investment funds into the United States from overseas is likely to result from

(A) expectations for reduced U.S. economic growth.

(B) a growing instability in the U.S. dollar value.

(C) a growing belief among investors that the U.S. dollar is overvalued.

(D) a rise in U.S. interest rates relative to world interest rates.

(E) an increase in the U.S. inflation rate.

49. The Open Market Committee of the Federal Reserve System (the Fed) is the committee that

(A) administers FDIC and FSLIC for member banks.

(B) provides advice on banking policy to the Fed.

(C) monitors regulatory banking laws for member banks.

(D) sets policy on the sale and purchase of government bonds by the Fed.

(E) follows the actions and operations of financial markets to keep them open and competitive.

50. If bond prices increase, then their

    (A) interest rate will decrease.

    (B) interest rate will increase.

    (C) transactions demand for money will decrease.

    (D) transactions demand for money will increase.

    (E) asset demand has decreased.

51. A demand deposit at a commercial bank is

    (A) an asset to a bank and a liability to the Fed.

    (B) a liability to the depositor and an asset to the bank.

    (C) a liability to both the depositor and the bank.

    (D) an asset to the depositor and a liability to the bank.

    (E) an asset to both the depositor and the bank.

52. An individual deposits $10,000 in a commercial bank. The bank is required to hold 20 percent of all deposits on reserve at the regional Federal Reserve Bank. The deposit increases the loan capacity of the bank by

    (A) $11,000.

    (B) $10,800.

    (C) $9,600.

    (D) $8,000.

    (E) $6,000.

53. If the required reserve ratio is 20 percent, the effective monetary multiplier for the banking system will be

    (A) 2.

    (B) 3.

    (C) 4.

(D) 5.

(E) 6.

54. The primary mission of monetary policy is to assist the economy in achieving

   (A) a rapid pace of economic growth.

   (B) an interest rate that constantly supports business investment.

   (C) a money supply based on the gold standard.

   (D) price stability, economic growth, and full employment level of total output.

   (E) a balanced budget consistent with full employment.

55. If the Fed buys government bonds from commercial banks in the open market

   (A) the Fed gives the bonds to the commercial banks, and they pay for them by writing checks that increase their reserves at the Fed.

   (B) the banks give the bonds to the Fed, which then increases the reserves of the banks, thereby encouraging higher interest rates.

   (C) the Fed gives the bonds to the commercial banks, and they pay for them by writing checks that decrease their reserves at the Fed.

   (D) commercial banks give the bonds to the Fed, which then pays for them by increasing the reserves of the commercial banks, thereby encouraging lower interest rates.

   (E) commercial banks give the bonds to the Fed, and it pays for them by decreasing the money supply.

56. If the Fed sells government bonds to the public in the open market,

   (A) the Fed gives the bonds to the public; the public pays for the bonds by writing a check that (when cleared) will increase the money supply.

(B) the Fed gives the bonds to the public; the public pays for them by writing checks that (when cleared) will decrease commercial bank reserves at the Fed, raising interest rates.

(C) banks buy the bonds from people, increasing the money supply and lowering interest rates.

(D) the public gives the bonds to the Fed; the Fed pays for the bonds by check, which (when deposited) decreases the money supply.

(E) the public gives the bonds to the Fed; the Fed pays for the bonds by check, which (when deposited) increases interest rates.

57. Assume that the required reserve ratio for commercial banks is 20 percent. If the Federal Reserve Banks buy $5 billion in government securities from commercial banks, the lending ability of the banking system will

(A) decrease by $9 billion.

(B) increase by $9 billion.

(C) increase by $15 billion.

(D) increase by $20 billion.

(E) increase by $25 billion.

Id and AD

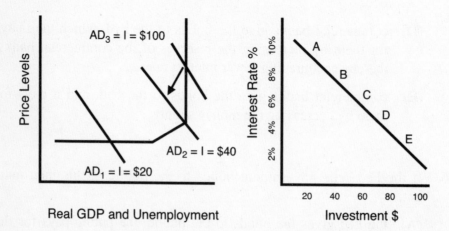

58. Refer to the preceding models, in which the numbers after the AD_1, AD_2, and AD_3 labels indicate the level of investment spending associated with each AD curve. All numbers are in billions of dollars. The interest rate and the level of investment spending in the economy are at point E on the investment demand curve. To achieve noninflationary, full employment output in the economy, the monetary authorities should

    (A) decrease AD by increasing the interest rate from 2 to 4 percent.

    (B) decrease AD by increasing the interest rate from 4 to 6 percent.

    (C) increase AD by decreasing the interest rate from 4 to 2 percent.

    (D) increase the level of investment spending from $100 billion to $150 billion.

    (E) increase interest rates to 8% and reduce AD_3 to AD_2.

59. Which of the following is the most accurate description of events when monetary authorities increase the size of commercial banks' excess reserves?

    (A) A fall in interest rates decreases the money supply, causing an increase in investment spending, output, and employment.

    (B) The money supply is increased, which decreases the interest rate and causes investment spending, output, and employment to increase.

    (C) A rise in interest rates increases the money supply, causing a decrease in investment spending, output, and employment.

    (D) The money supply is decreased, which increases the interest rate and causes investment spending, output, and employment to decrease.

    (E) Bond prices fall, interest rates increase, investment spending rises, and employment and GDP increase.

60. Assume that demand-pull inflationary pressure is a growing problem for the economy. In response to this threat, the Federal Reserve decides to pursue a policy to reduce the inflationary pressure. At the same time, Congress decides to eliminate a budget surplus. Which set of policy changes by the Fed and Congress would result, thereby offsetting each other?

	Monetary Policy	**Fiscal Policy**
(A)	selling government securities	lowering taxes
(B)	buying government securities	increasing spending
(C)	selling government bonds	raising taxes
(D)	buying government bonds	increasing subsidies
(E)	selling government bonds	increasing spending

AP Macroeconomics

TEST

Section II

Planning Time: 10 minutes
Writing Time: 50 minutes

DIRECTIONS: You have fifty minutes to answer all three of the following questions. It is suggested that you spend approximately half your time on the first question and divide the remaining time equally between the next two. In answering these questions, you should emphasize the line of reasoning that generated your results; it is not enough to list the results of your analysis. Include correctly labeled diagrams, if useful or required, in explaining your answers. A correctly labeled diagram must have all axes and curves labeled and must show directional changes.

---

1. Suppose that the U.S. economy is at full employment and experiencing hyperinflation.

   (a) Draw a correctly labeled aggregate demand and aggregate supply model, depicting the price level, GDP, income, and employment equilibrium of the current economy.

   (b) Congress, which has been allowing a large budget deficit in prior years, reacts to the current state of the economy by maintaining the current spending level while raising personal income taxes to an amount equal to the amount spent. What reaction would an economist express regarding this balanced-budget proposal? Justify your answer.

   (c) Explain how this increase in household income tax would, in the short run, affect each of the following sectors:

        (i)   household consumption

        (ii)   business gross investment

        (iii) imports

        (iv) exports

(d)   Given the same economic conditions, describe the action the Federal Reserve would take. Use the aggregate demand/aggregate supply model to analyze the impact of this policy on each of the following areas:

        (i)   interest rates

        (ii)   business gross investment

        (iii) output and employment

2.   The First National Bank of Buffalo sells $10,000 worth of government bonds to the Federal Reserve Bank of New York. The reserve ratio requirement is 20%.

(a)   Explain the impact of this transaction on each of the following.

        (i)   What is the maximum amount of new loans that First National Bank can issue?

        (ii)   What will be the total impact on the nation's money supply?

        (iii) How do banking actions of this nature affect interest rates?

(b)   List two actions in the economy that might reduce the impact of First National's transaction.

3.   Assume that the United States and Germany are the only two countries engaged in trade, with a floating exchange currency rate (dollars and marks), and that they trade two goods, beef and beer.

(a)   If the U.S. demand for beer increased while the German demand for beef remained constant, how would each of the following be affected?

        (i)   demand for marks

    (ii)   trade value of the dollar

(b)   If interest rates, at the same time, decreased in the United States while German rates remained constant, how would that change affect each of the following?

    (i)   trade value of the dollar

    (ii)   supply of dollars in the currency exchange market

AP Economics

Macroeconomics Test

ANSWER KEY

Section I

1.	(E)	16.	(B)	31.	(E)	46.	(E)
2.	(D)	17.	(D)	32.	(E)	47.	(B)
3.	(B)	18.	(D)	33.	(C)	48.	(D)
4.	(B)	19.	(C)	34.	(B)	49.	(D)
5.	(A)	20.	(D)	35.	(B)	50.	(A)
6.	(B)	21.	(B)	36.	(B)	51.	(D)
7.	(D)	22.	(C)	37.	(C)	52.	(D)
8.	(C)	23.	(B)	38.	(E)	53.	(D)
9.	(D)	24.	(D)	39.	(C)	54.	(D)
10.	(E)	25.	(D)	40.	(D)	55.	(D)
11.	(D)	26.	(A)	41.	(D)	56.	(B)
12.	(B)	27.	(E)	42.	(E)	57.	(E)
13.	(C)	28.	(A)	43.	(D)	58.	(E)
14.	(C)	29.	(A)	44.	(E)	59.	(B)
15.	(D)	30.	(C)	45.	(D)	60.	(A)

DETAILED EXPLANATIONS OF ANSWERS

Macroeconomics Test

Section I

1. **(E)** Answers A through D all involve movements along or a return to the original PPF curve. Remember that if the curve is to shift outward, economic growth must take place. This means that an increase in one or all of the factors of production must occur (increased raw materials, labor, investment goods, or innovation). If cereal making is more efficient, the relationship between inputs of production and the resulting output has improved. You are getting increased cereal production with less input.

2. **(D)** An economic trade-off occurs when you have two g/s whose inputs are interchangeable and limited. Therefore, there must be a reduction in the output of one g/s (education) in order to increase the output of the alternative g/s (military). A government's resources are limited; it can devote those resources, in various combinations, to construction of military goods or to education goods.

3. **(B)** Scarcity, by definition, describes the nature of our existence. This simply means that resources are finite when compared to humanity's infinite needs and wants. Scarcity is the driving force behind the creation of all economic systems.

4. **(B)** Specialization—producing the g/s that you are most efficient in—applies both to the individual and to nations as a whole. Division of labor results in greater overall production, thereby increasing the general wealth. Comparative advantage reveals the economic truth that even though one producer may have superior efficiency when compared to another, both benefit from increased productivity when the less efficient producer focuses on its strength, while the more efficient producer specializes in the alternative good.

5. **(A)** Comparative advantage demonstrates the efficiency that results from specialization. As individuals or nations specialize, their output relative to their input increases. Therefore, the total combined output for these countries increases. This increase in goods increases the standard of living of both nations.

6. **(B)** GDP is the total dollar value of all finished goods and services sold in the product market. This is done so that there is no double-counting.

7. **(D)** The consumer price index (CPI) measures the price change in a fixed basket of goods and services. The prices are compared to those of an established base (index) year; it does not measure from the previous year. This allows more accurate inflation measurement over long periods of time. One of the main criticisms of this tool is that it overestimates inflation, in part because the basket is fixed so that new g/s are excluded and original g/s that may no longer be in demand are retained.

8. **(C)** In the formula to determine GDP, $C + I_g + G + X_n$, I_g represents the gross investment in capital goods by a firm. Therefore, any expenditure that adds to the future productivity of the firm is classified as an investment. Repurchasing stock in the firm does not alter productivity, so it is not an expenditure on investment.

9. **(D)** One way to determine GDP is by summing all the expenditures on output. The same data can be compiled by adding all the components of income (in the end, they should be equal). On the expenditure side of GDP, all final goods and services are bought by four sectors. The three domestic sectors are: household consumption (C), business investment (I), and government spending (G). The other component of expenditure is foreign (X) purchase of U.S. g/s minus U.S. purchases of foreign product or exports minus imports (X_n). Therefore, the expenditure formula for determining GDP is $C + I_g + G + X_n$.

10. **(E)** The expansion phase of the business cycle means, by definition, that the output of the economy (GDP) is increasing. By the very nature of GDP, an increase must mean that employment of inputs is also increasing; as labor is a main input, its employment is also increasing. Since output equals income, if output is increasing then income must also be increasing. Price levels will also begin to rise at

some point (stage 2 intermediate). However, if the economy is in deep recession (stage 1 horizontal), output can increase without price rise, as we are using so few inputs that increasing opportunity costs have not begun to have an effect on cost and thus price.

11. **(D)** A decrease in aggregate demand results in a change in aggregate supply quantity. If consumption of autos declines, then the quantity of steel supplied, as an intermediate good, would also decline. If output declines, then jobs and income must also decline.

12. **(B)** Structural unemployment, by definition, is the result of a mismatch of skills or location. This is a mismatch of job skills, as the robot has replaced the worker.

13. **(C)** Full employment does not mean 100% employment. By the very definition of structural and frictional unemployment, there will always be unemployed people. Therefore, to determine the unemployment due to a downturn in the business cycle, it is necessary to discount the structurally and frictionally unemployed.

14. **(C)** The second stage of the AS curve, as one moves rightward, represents diminishing marginal productivity and increasing opportunity costs that lead to rising price levels. If we reduce the aggregate demand, the AD curve moves inward, resulting in lower output, employment, and disposable income. These changes would result in overall lower price levels. Also, as fewer resource inputs are required by producers, marginal productivity would actually increase, cost per unit would decline, and a lower price would be charged.

15. **(D)** The vertical stage three of AS represents an economy that has reached maximum productivity. All resource inputs are being used. Therefore, any increase in aggregate demand cannot be met with increased production. Because demand has increased while supply has remained fixed, a higher price level results. This is sometimes referred to as "hyperinflation," as the rise in prices in this environment can be very large.

AD/AS

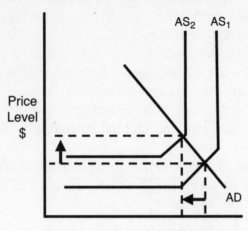

GDP, Income, and Employment

16. **(B)**   Transportation input is a variable cost of supply. As more transportation is used, the cost per unit produced increases. An increase in marginal costs would be represented by a shift inward and upward of the AS curve as MC equals the supply curve. In the short run AD would remain fixed, so the result would be a decrease in output (GDP) and a rise in prices.

17. **(D)**   Keynes challenged the long-held assumption of Classical economists that long-run AS is perfectly inelastic. They reasoned that price levels, output, and employment were self-regulating. Keynes argued that an economy can become fixed in a cycle of long-run recession, from which it will recover only if stimulated. Keynes argued that by increasing spending and cutting taxes (budget deficit) to the household, the C element of aggregate expenditure will stimulate expansion in the economy.

18. **(D)**   By definition, the factor market is where firms purchase the inputs of production. In a free market, individual households own the input factors. Firms pay input owners, which is the household income. The product market, by definition, is where firms sell the finished product to individual households. The product market is the revenue source for firms, and households expend their income in consuming those g/s.

19. **(C)**   Income has a direct relationship to aggregate expenditure. If disposable income increases, then expenditure also increases in relation to the MPC.

Aggregate Expenditure and Disposable Income

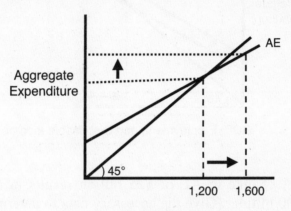

20. **(D)**   Bonds are an investment alternative to holding cash. Remember that inflation erodes the value of currency over time. Bonds (corporate and government) are promissory notes whereby the buyer loans money to the seller in exchange for repayment of the loaned amount (principal) plus a set interest rate of return at a set date of maturity. The risk in this investment is that the buyer foregoes the current purchasing power of the currency, in the belief that the interest payment will more than cover any inflation that might occur over the length of the bond maturity—hence the speculatory nature of the investment.

21. **(B)**   When interest rates fall (8% to 2%) and business expectations change, a shift in investment demand (Id to Id_1) will stimulate an increase in the I_g component of AE (AE to AE_1).

Interest Rates, I$_g$, and AE

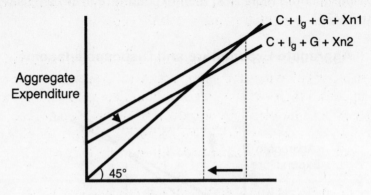

GDP, Employment, and Disposable Income

22. **(C)** A change in AE of $25 billion results in an increase in output of $100 billion. [Give the necessary data to determine the MPC/MPS and the multiplier]. Since an AE change of 25 yields a 100 change in output, the multiplier is 4 (25 × 4 = 100). To have a multiplier of 4, the MPS must be 0.25 and the MPC 0.75. This is so because 1/MPS (1/0.25 = 4) = the multiplier and 1 − MPS (1 − 0.25 = 0.75) = MPC.

23. **(B)** Exports, as a component of AE, are an injection into the economy. If exports fell and all else remained equal, the AE would decrease and the equilibrium level of GDP would decrease.

Interest Rates, I$_g$, and AE

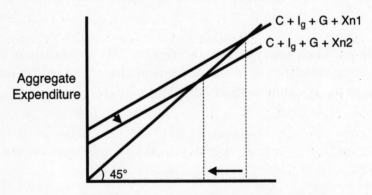

GDP, Employment, and Disposable Income

24. **(D)**   The injection-leakage analysis of AE/GDP considers, by definition, leakages to consist of savings, taxes, and imports. All three items represent no spending in the domestic economy.

25. **(D)**   [This question tests knowledge of the unique relationship of tax, consumer behavior, and change in AE.] Consumers will react to taxes by adjusting their savings in an amount determined by their MPS. Tax increases will be offset by a reduction in savings. In this case, a $40 billion dollar tax levy would be compensated for, by consumers, through a reduction in savings of $10 billion ($40 \times 0.25 = 10$).

26. **(A)**   [This question follows up the concept discussed in question 25.] The reaction of consumers to a tax increase, which is then subject to the multiplier, explains what is known as the balanced budget multiplier. This gap is always equal to a factor of 1. In other words, any equal combination of spending increase and tax increase ($100 million spending and $100 million tax increase adds $100 million to the GDP), will always result in that amount added to the economy. This is because government spending is subject to the full multiplier, whereas taxes are first reduced by the MPS and then subject to the multiplier. Thus, a recessionary or inflationary gap always results from equal amounts of spending and tax quantities.

27. **(E)**   The multiplier is 4. The formula to determine the multiplier is:

$$\frac{\text{change in real GDP}}{\text{change in spending}}, \text{ so } \frac{1,600-1,200}{400\pm300}=\frac{400}{100}=4$$

28. **(A)** $1,200 billion. If this is a closed economy without a government sector, the aggregate expenditure would be 300 and the multiplier would remain at 4; $300 \times 4 = 1,200$.

29. **(A)**   Purchase of imports is a leakage from domestic aggregate expenditure, so it would cause X_n to decrease. If AE falls from AE_1 to AE_2, then so does AD, from AD_1 to AD_2. As AD decreases so do price levels (depending on relationship to AS stage), employment, and GDP. This can be seen in the following graphic depiction:

Decline in AD/AS and AE

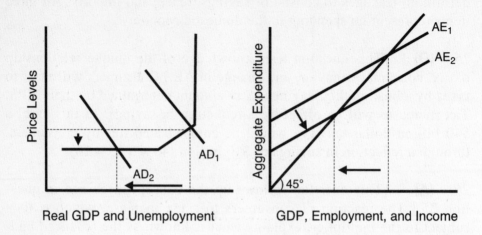

Real GDP and Unemployment   GDP, Employment, and Income

30. **(C)** An increase in the money supply would put more income into the aggregate expenditure. This in turn would increase the aggregate demand. A decrease in interest rates would also help to stimulate aggregate demand, as lower rates encourage borrowing and spending. Both activities stimulate an economy.

31. **(E)** Business investment is a component of AE and thus has a direct influence on AD. If the other three elements of AE remained constant and I_g decreased, then AE would move downward and the AD would move inward. This is depicted in the two models above. Notice that price levels, GDP, and employment all decrease.

32. **(E)** Technology affects productivity. A technical improvement would by definition increase productivity, thereby lowering costs. A lowering of costs and increased productivity shifts the AS curve outward. This outward shift serves to decrease prices, increase output, increase income, and create employment. This could be summed up as an increase in the overall standard of living. The following model shows this event graphically:

Increase in AS

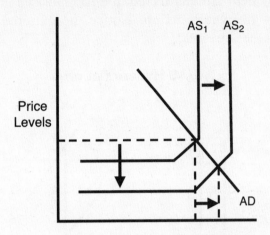

GDP, Income, and Employment

33. **(C)** If firms experienced an unplanned and rapid decrease in inventories, this means that AD has shifted to the right. A large increase in the money supply occurred and there are few additional g/s with which to immediately replace depleted inventories. When money enters the economy while few g/s enter, inflation is by definition a result. Also notice that in the AD/AS model, as you enter stages 2 and 3, price levels rise.

34. **(B)** In the short run, supply is fixed. If government increases spending while at the same time cutting taxes, the AE will increase, causing the AD to increase (move to the right). This change in AD causes an increase in employment and an increase in price levels.

Increase in AD/AS and AE

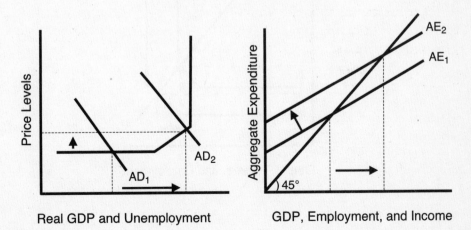

Real GDP and Unemployment   GDP, Employment, and Income

35. **(B)** If AD increases and as a result price levels rise, while GDP and employment are unaffected, the AD must be in stage 3 of the AS. This results in hyperinflation. Notice the extreme rise in prices that results from these events.

AD/AS Hyperinflation

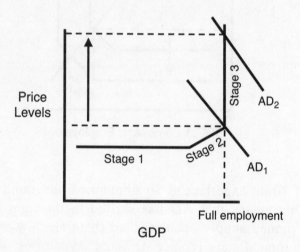

36. **(B)** For that combination to occur in the economy, the AS must have moved inward. When there is a supply shock, there is an unexpected increase in input prices, price levels rise, and GDP and employment decline.

Decrease in AS

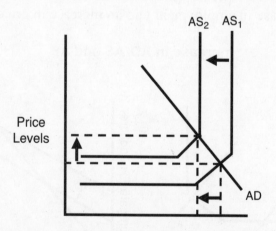

37. **(C)** Keynes advocated government intervention in the business cycle to manage the economy in an attempt to moderate the extremes of the business cycle. Through fiscal policy, the government can counter the cycle, stimulating during recession and contracting during expansion. So, if inflation were occurring because of an AD that is too high, the government could cause a contraction in the consumption segment of AD by increasing taxes and reducing government spending.

Decrease in Aggregate Expenditure

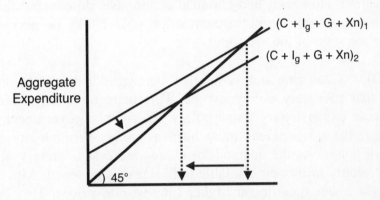

GDP, Employment, and Disposable Income

38. **(E)** [The basis for this answer involves a knowledge of both the multiplier and the realization that a change in tax is partially absorbed by the marginal propensity to save (prior to the effect of the multiplier).] With an MPC of 0.75, the MPS is 0.25; therefore, the initial tax change must be reduced by 0.25. A tax raise of *$16 billion* would first be offset by a $4 billion reduction in household savings. The remainder of $12 billion (16 − 4 = 12) is then subject to the multiplier, which is 4 because it equals 1/MPS (1/0.25 = 4). A $12 billion net tax would reduce the household consumption component of GDP by $48 billion (12 × 4 = 48).

39. **(C)** Automatic stabilizers increase or decrease with expansion and contraction of the economy. Examples of automatic stabilizers are unemployment insurance and Temporary Assistance to Needy Families (TANF). Tax revenues also change automatically, in a direct relationship with the business cycle. If GDP rises, tax revenues increase and transfer payments decline. Conversely, as GDP declines, tax revenues decrease and transfer payments increase. Therefore, automatic stabilizers produce a cyclically adjusted budget.

40. **(D)**   There are many criticisms of fiscal policy. The main one is the time lags that occur in the recognition, construction, and operational impact of that policy on the business cycle. Another is that the degree of economic influence desired (great or small stimulus/contraction) is difficult to judge (fiscal policy can be like trying to swat a mosquito with a sledge hammer). Many times fiscal policy of an expansionary nature begins to have an impact long after the recession has passed. This is the advantage that monetary policy enjoys over fiscal policy, both in the almost immediate impact and the degree of influence desired. However, neo-classical economists do contend that both monetary and fiscal stimulus/contraction power may be necessary to manage the state of the economy.

41. **(D)**   Crowding out is another damaging side effect of fiscal policy that monetary policy avoids. This happens when government pursues an expansionary fiscal policy. To finance government deficit spending, the government must borrow money through the sale of Treasury bonds. As the demand for money increases, interest rates rise and the supply of money available to business is lessened. Also, I_g will demand a lower quantity at higher interest-rate prices. This is obviously counterproductive from an injection-leakage analysis, as the decrease in I_g would partially offset the increase in G. So, as the following diagram shows, interest rates would rise from 4% to 8%, reducing the I_g component of AE. The AD/AS model demonstrates the intended results of fiscal policy, moving AD_1 to AD_2 with the actual lessened impact AD_1 to AD_{2a}, due to crowding out. Most economists contend, however, that this crowding-out effect would be rendered irrelevant during recession if the Federal Reserve cooperated with an easing of money policy.

Crowding Out

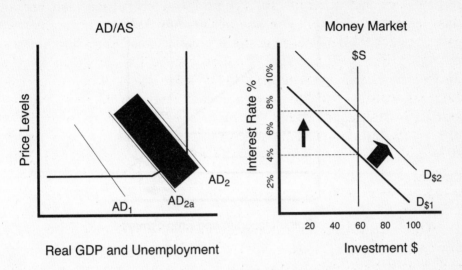

AD/AS

Price Levels

Real GDP and Unemployment

AD$_1$ AD$_{2a}$ AD$_2$

Money Market

$S

Interest Rate %

2% 4% 6% 8% 10%

D$_{$2}$

D$_{$1}$

20   40   60   80   100

Investment $

42. **(E)** When Congress pursues a contractionary fiscal policy, it reduces spending and increases taxes. The result of this behavior is to decrease the money supply. This causes interest rates to rise, discouraging households from purchasing g/s (both domestic and foreign). Initially, the weak dollar (due to inflation) coupled with stronger foreign currencies results in exports rising while imports fall. Thus, the X_n component of AE/AD increases and partially offsets the decrease in the C, I_g, and G components. In the long run, the higher interest rates attract foreign investors and the increased demand for the dollar causes it to appreciate, reversing the trade balance trend (long-run trade equilibrium concept).

43. **(D)** Supply-side economists contend that tax reductions aimed at the I_g will promote increases in productivity and thus output, along with job creation and higher income. This is attained without inflation because the increase in income is equal to the increase in output. This is a revisit of Say's Law. Many economists are critical of the degree to which tax cuts affect investment and thus AS expansion. Some contend that the lower tax rates only serve to enhance the wealth of business owners and further distort income distribution. This area continues to be investigated by economists for evidence of some impact of tax policy on AS expansion.

Increase in AS

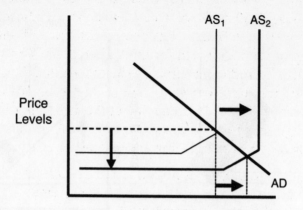

Output, Income, and Employment

44. **(E)**   If foreign demand for dollars to deposit into U.S. money markets increases (D_1 to D_2), then the value of the dollar will appreciate, because the foreign currencies would depreciate (5 to 7.5 foreign currency units per dollar).

The Currency Money Market

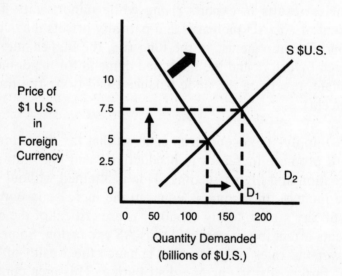

Quantity Demanded
(billions of $U.S.)

45. **(D)**   [This answer is based on the principle of comparative advantage.] Total output for two nations will be greatest when each good is produced by the one that has the lower domestic opportunity cost for that good. This is determined by calculating the ratio of the domestic

opportunity cost. In the case of Brazil and the United States, the United States must give up 100 units of wheat to get 200 cellular phones (2cp = 1w). For Brazil, 50 units of wheat must be sacrificed to gain 200 phones (2cp = 0.5w). Brazil has the lower cost of producing cell phones, since 1cp = 0.25 w and for the United States 1cp = 0.5 w. Both benefit by Brazil producing phones and the United States producing wheat and then trading. Both gain from specializing. If we assume that both nations were separately producing at the midpoint of their production possibilities, they would create the following scenario. They have 25 more units of wheat than before specialization.

Country	Before Specialization	After Specialization	Net Change	Gains from Trade
United States	100 cell phones	0 cell phones	−100 cell phones	0 cell phone
	50 wheat	100 wheat	+ 50 wheat	+ 25 wheat
Brazil	100 cell phones	200 cell phones	+100 cell phones	
	25 wheat	0 wheat	− 25 wheat	

46. **(E)** [This answer is based on comparative advantage analysis, as shown in the answer to question 45, and adding the terms of trade principle.] After specialization, countries will want more goods than they had prior to it. They must receive a ratio of return greater than they had from their domestic production. In this case, Nigeria (3 cocoa for 1 banana) produces bananas and Colombia (5 cocoa for 1 banana) produces cocoa. Nigeria will want to get more than its domestic return of 3 cocoa for 1 banana (say, 4 cocoa for 1 banana +1), which increases its standard of living. Colombia will want to get a greater return than its domestic production of 1 banana for 5 cocoa (say, 1.25 banana for 5 cocoa).

47. **(B)** "Dumping" is when a nation (or firm) sells a good below cost as a means of harming its competition. Under the rules established by the WTO, countries found guilty of dumping goods in another nation's market may be penalized by the WTO, which may allow the offended nation to place a tariff on the foreign producer's good as a remedy. This tax punishes the offending nation and returns the field to a competitive market.

48. **(D)** If interest rates rose in the United States, the higher rate of return on invested money would attract foreign investors. Because they have to exchange their foreign currency into dollars to purchase U.S. securities, the demand for U.S. dollars would increase. If the demand for dollars increased, the value of the dollar would appreciate (see model for question 44).

49. **(D)** The FOMC is the monetary policy-making branch of the Federal Reserve system. Its membership of five Fed bank presidents and the seven members of the Board of Governors meets approximately every six weeks to set the discount rate and the federal funds rate. The federal funds rate is attained through the sale or purchase of Treasury bonds in the open market.

50. **(A)** Critical to FOMC policy is the indirect relationship that exists between bond prices and their interest yield. When bond prices rise (say, due to increased demand), the interest rate yield on those bonds declines. If the FOMC increases the money supply by purchasing bonds, their yield would decline (as would interest rates—easy money). If the Fed decreases the money supply by selling bonds, their yield would increase (as would interest rates—tight money).

51. **(D)** By definition, a deposit at a bank is placed on the bank's books as a liability, as this is money that is owed by the bank to the depositor. The deposit is an asset to the depositor, as it represents value owned by the depositor.

52. **(D)** This function is at the heart of the fractional reserve banking system. The Federal Reserve sets a reserve ratio requirement for member banks. Reserves in excess of this required amount are available for loan. In this case, the reserve is 20%; if $10,000 is deposited, then $2,000 is reserved with the Fed and $8,000 is available to loan.

53. **(D)** Because loan proceeds are deposited by the recipients into their banks, that action adds to the reserves of that depository. The additional deposit, after the reserve ratio is met, increases the depository's assets and the money is re-loaned. This is known as the money multiplier. The formula is 1/reserve ratio requirement. In this case, the rrr is 0.20, so the multiplier is 5 (1/0.20 = 5).

54. **(D)**   The established mission of the Federal Reserve and its monetary policy is to achieve price stability, an environment conducive to economic growth, and full employment.

55. **(D)**   When the FOMC orders bonds to be purchased from commercial banks, the bond is given to the Fed in exchange for a credit to the reserves of the commercial bank. This credit enables the bank to increase its loans and thus the money supply. This increase in the money supply relative to the demand for money generally lowers interest rates, thereby encouraging expansion in the economy.

56. **(B)**   This action has the opposite impact of the action taken in question 55. When the Fed sells bonds, it removes money from circulation and replaces it with a bond. As money is removed from the market, available interest rates rise. Also, as the supply of bonds in the bond market increases, their price decreases. As mentioned earlier, this increases their interest rate yield.

57. **(E)**   If the reserve is 20 percent, the multiplier is 5 ($1/0.20 = 5$). If $5 billion is added to commercial bank reserves, 5 times that amount would eventually enter the economy ($5 billion $\times$ 5 = 25).

58. **(E)**   The current interest rates are too expansionary and as a result the economy is in hyperinflation. From the money market model, it is clear that at I = $40 billion, the interest rate is 8%. The higher interest rate would tighten money, slow expenditure, and move AD back to stage 2.

Id and AD/AS

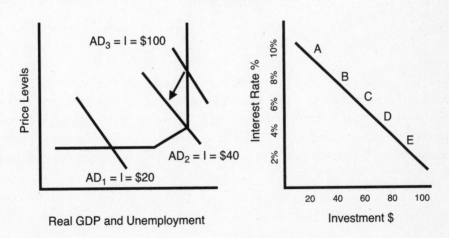

Price Levels / Real GDP and Unemployment

$AD_3 = I = \$100$

$AD_2 = I = \$40$

$AD_1 = I = \$20$

Interest Rate %

Investment $

59. (B)   [This question again focuses on the relationship between interest rates, I_g, AE, AD, and GDP.] In this case, monetary policy has been one of easy money (\$S1 to \$S2) that encourages (interest rates 10% to 4%) business investment (\$20 to \$80), thus increasing the AE/AD (AD$_1$ to AD$_2$) and stimulating expansion of the economy. When output increases, so too do employment and income.

Fed "Easy Money" Policy
The Money Market and AD/AS

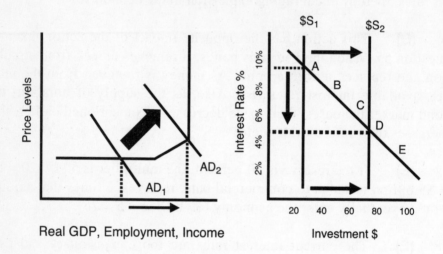

60. (A)   The monetary policy of selling government securities would reduce the money supply, increase interest rates, and reduce the I_g component of AE/AD. This would be contractionary in nature. This reduction of expenditure would be offset by a fiscal policy of lowering taxes, which would increase income, increase AE/AD, and be expansionary in nature.

DETAILED EXPLANATIONS OF ANSWERS

Macroeconomics Test

Section II

1.　(a)　The economy depicted by AD_2/AS portrays hyperinflation. Notice that no additional g/s can be produced, as we are at our maximum short-run production possibilities frontier. Thus, any increase in AD (AD_1 to AD_2) only serves to cause massive inflation of price levels.

AD/AS Hyperinflation

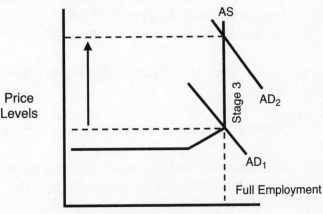

(b)　This change in the relationship between spending (injection) and taxation (leakage) would be an improvement over the prior years of deficit spending, as it is an expansionary policy employed to combat recession. However, an economist would criticize this policy as failing to account for the inflationary budget gap that would occur. When spending and taxation are equal, a budget gap (factor of 1) results, because households will account for a portion (equal to the MPS, with the balance then subject to the multiplier) of their tax by reducing their savings. Because government spending is subject to the full multiplier, an injection of money thus results from the imbalance. This policy will expand the money supply and generate even more inflation. This fiscal policy will not halt the hyperinflation.

(c) (i) It would decrease disposable income, thereby reducing the consumption component of AE/AD. The effect would be moderated by the reduction in MPS.

(ii) The reduction in household spending would decrease business investment, thereby reducing the I_g component of AE/AD.

(iii) The decrease in disposable income would reduce spending on imports.

The decreased demand for money would cause interest rates to decrease and the dollar to depreciate in value.

The dollar's devaluation in currency markets would further increase the price of foreign goods to America, further decreasing the demand for imports.

(iv) Lower domestic price levels would cause exports to increase.

Short-run depreciated dollars would increase exports.

Reduction in the transaction demand for money would cause interest rates to decrease, and the foreign demand for dollars for investment purposes would decrease, leading to additional devaluation.

(d) The Fed would pursue a contractionary monetary policy and decrease the money supply. The decrease in the money supply through the sale of government bonds would cause interest rates (federal funds rate) to rise, which would reduce both the consumer and business investment components of aggregate expenditure and thereby cause aggregate demand to decrease, as seen by the shift of AD_2 to AD_1. This would lower price levels and combat inflation.

FOMC "Tight Money Policy"

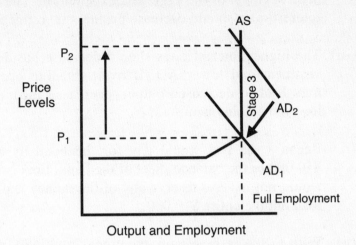

Output and Employment

(i) The tightening of the money supply ($S\$_1$ to $S\$_2$) through the sale of government bonds by the Fed would raise interest rates (ir_1 to ir_2). The higher price of money would cause the quantity demanded of money to decrease (Q_1 to Q_2). The decrease in money borrowed and expended would cause the AD to decrease, as depicted in the preceding "tight money" figure.

The Money Market and FOMC Sale of Bonds

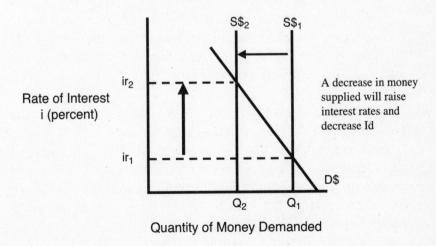

Quantity of Money Demanded

(ii) FOMC policy is aimed at the business gross investment segment of the aggregate expenditure. The higher interest rates should decrease business investment.

(iii) The higher interest rates should decrease business investment and lower AD. If overtightening occurs, it may lead to decreased output, decreased income, and lowered employment.

2. (a) (i) Because the Fed would pay for the bond by adding $10,000 to the balance sheet of the bank, First National would not have to reserve any of the money and could loan out the entire $10,000.

(ii) With a 20% reserve ratio, the money multiplier will be 5. Assuming that all the banks loan out all their excess reserves and that no leakages occur, the money supply would increase by $50,000. This "easy money" policy would expand the money supply and the AD, leading to increased output and employment.

(iii) As indicated in the preceding response, the increase in the money supply would serve to lower interest rates (ir_1 to ir_2) and increase the quantity of money demanded (Q_1 to Q_2). The Money Market model graphically portrays this action.

Money Market

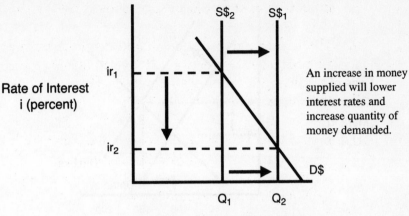

An increase in money supplied will lower interest rates and increase quantity of money demanded.

Quantity of Money Demanded

(b) (i) If businesses and consumers have negative expectations about the future state of the economy, they may choose not to borrow money. This would reduce the impact of the increased money supply at lower interest rates.

(ii) Banks might decide to hold excess reserves and not make loans.

or

Businesses or consumers might decide to increase their currency holdings.

3. (a) (i) The U.S. demand for marks (D_{marks1} to D_{marks2}) would increase to pay for the greater quantity of beer imported. Remember, the Germans would want to be paid in marks.

Currency Money Market

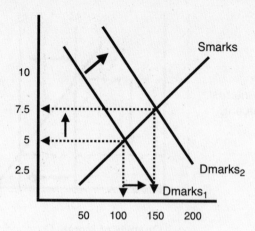

Price of 1
German
Mark in
U.S. $

Amount of Marks Demanded
(billions of U.S. dollars)

(ii) As seen in the preceding model, the price of the mark in dollars would increase ($5.00 per mark to $7.50 per mark). This would mean that the dollar had depreciated in value. It takes more dollars to buy German beer.

(b) (i) If interest rates declined, the quantity of dollars demanded in the economy would increase. This would be inflationary, thus further eroding the value of the dollar. Also, lower interest rates would discourage German investment in the U.S. economy, thus reducing the German demand for dollars and contributing to further weakening of the dollar. In the end, these outcomes would dampen U.S. enthusiasm for German beer, make German beer relatively more expensive to Americans, and reduce U.S. imports.

The Money Market and Lower Interest Rates

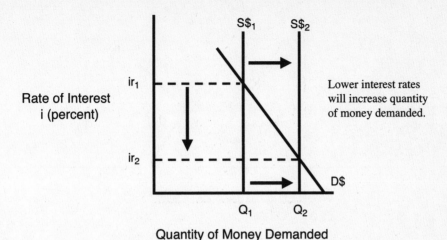

Rate of Interest
i (percent)

Lower interest rates
will increase quantity
of money demanded.

Quantity of Money Demanded

(ii)   The supply of U.S. dollars into the currency market
would increase ($S_{\$us1}$ to $S_{\$us2}$). This would further
weaken the international value of the dollar (0.20
marks per dollar to 0.13 marks per dollar). The cheaper
dollar would increase the German quantity demanded.
In the long run (trade equilibrium), the appreciation of
the German mark would increase the German demand
for imported beef as it became relatively cheaper.

The Currency Money Market

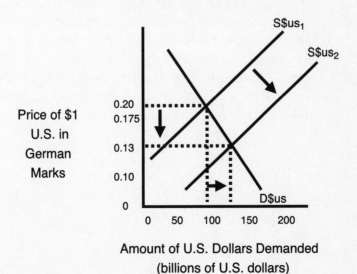

Price of $1
U.S. in
German
Marks

Amount of U.S. Dollars Demanded
(billions of U.S. dollars)

▼
APPENDICES

APPENDIX A

ADDITIONAL MICRO AND MACRO SECTION II FREE-RESPONSE TOPICS FOR STUDY

1. MICROECONOMICS

I. Labor market analysis based on a table that requires the student to determine MRP = MRC at various prices and costs
    1. Knowledge of purely competitive labor market; firm to industry determination of wage

II. A firm is a natural monopoly without government price regulations
    1. Draw the appropriate model
    2. Government regulations applied; draw new model
    3. Long-run impact upon the firm (normal profit, economic profit, loss and shutdown knowledge)

III. Use of marginal analysis
    1. Derive supply curve
    2. Least-cost combination of labor and capital
    3. Regulate an industry with negative externalities

2. MICROECONOMICS

I. Competitive firms are in a market where demand and supply is price inelastic, but not perfectly so. They operate in the inelastic portions.
    1. Supply increases impact on price, quantity, and revenue; draw model
    2. Cost and demand increases impact price and output quantity; draw model
    3. Government imposes a price floor impact on surplus and allocative efficiency

II. Total Productivity Table
    1. Diminishing marginal returns
    2. Relationship of average product curve to marginal product and average variable cost curve

III. Price discrimination between two customer groups with firms having constant cost
1. Role of elasticity of demand on prices
2. Profit maximization for the two consumer groups
3. Two conditions that must exist for the firms to be able to charge different prices

3. MICROECONOMICS

I. Two separate and purely competitive markets for a good produced by both the U.S. and foreign firms
1. Changes in supply curve of the U.S. as firms decrease and price increases
2. Textiles are close substitutes
3. Impact of a tariff on market price and quantity
4. Perfectly competitive labor market has a decrease in supply of labor and a wage rate increase; give impact; draw model

II. Two countries have different production possibilities
1. Identify comparative and absolute advantage
2. Predict specialization and effect of trade
3. Terms of exchange are analyzed

III. Contrast a purely competitive firm to a monopoly; draw market models

4. MICROECONOMICS

I. Analysis of market model for a monopoly
1. Profit maximization
2. Change to a purely competitive market
3. Allocative and productive efficiency
4. Impact of a government tax

II. Analysis of least-cost combination of inputs from a table with labor as a variable input
1. Type of market in which the firm sells its output
2. Type of labor market
3. MRP = MRC analysis determining quantity of labor inputs
4. Profit or loss level of the firm

III. Two separate and perfectly competitive markets with a domestic and foreign producer—they are close substitutes and demand is price elastic

1. Impact (price and output) of a tariff on foreign producer; draw model
2. Impact (price and output) of tariff on domestic producer; draw model

5. MICROECONOMICS

I. A purely competitive firm is in economic profit; draw model
   1. MR = MC analysis
   2. P = D = MR (price taker)
   3. Industry has downward sloping demand curve
   4. Economic profits attract firms to industry; show long-run normal profit

II. Spillover Costs exist
   1. Draw model showing current situation and socially optimum supply
   2. Government would move producers to allocative efficiency by a tax

III. Marginal Product Analysis Table
   1. Show maximization of worker inputs
   2. Law of Diminishing Returns; draw models
   3. Show where Marginal Product becomes negative

6. MICROECONOMICS

I. Contrast imperfectly competitive firm transition to a perfectly competitive environment.
   1. Output, price, and economic/normal profits
   2. Hiring labor in a perfectly competitive market

II. Negative Externality of air pollution and Spillover Benefits of military defense
   1. Allocation of resource using marginal benefit marginal cost analysis
   2. Government intervention
   3. Issue of privatization

III. Utility maximization analysis of apples and oranges; total utility table
   1. Price change impact on least-cost maximum utility combination of goods

7. MICROECONOMICS

I.   Firm is in a perfectly competitive market in short run economic profit
  1.   Side-by-side graphs to show the market and the firm
  2.   Economic profit area
  3.   Use models to show long run
  4.   Assume positive externalities are present; draw them on graph
  5.   Government policy that could promote socially optimum level of production

II. Draw a typical monopoly market model.
  1.   Relationship between a monopolist's demand and marginal revenue curve
  2.   Consumer surplus and deadweight loss

III. Assume a profit-maximizing firm that hires in a perfectly competitive labor market and sells in a perfectly competitive output market.
  1.   MRP of labor
  2.   Side-by-side models to show equilibrium wage, labor supply curve, and the number of workers hired
  3.   Firm develops a new technology that increases labor productivity and is not available to other firms
      a.   Impact on wage rates and number of workers hired

---

1. MACROECONOMICS

I.   Short 5% increase in the money supply
  1.   Impact of changes in interest rate on two countries with different elasticities of money demand; draw models
  2.   Identify the different impact monetary policy has on the two countries
  3.   Which is most like the U.S.?

II. Circular flow model without foreign sector
  1.   Draw and label it
  2.   Two ways to calculate its GDP
  3.   Identify AD and AS

III. Economy is in recession.
  1.   Monetary and fiscal policy action.

2. Show price and output changes; draw AD AS model
3. Show impact of policy changes on international value of the dollar

2. MACROECONOMICS

I. Full employment economy—government increases spending and incurs a greater deficit.
   1. Draw an AD/AS model showing this economy.
   2. Impact on long-run nominal and real interest rates
   3. Identify how tax policy could be used here to promote long-run growth.
   4. Use a PPF curve; identify capital goods versus consumption goods for this tax policy.

II. Federal Reserve System sells bonds in the open market.
   1. What happens to bank reserves and interest rates?
   2. What happens to the money market?
   3. Impact on economy; draw AD AS model

III. Labor productivity grows 3.2% annually, nominal wage is constant.
   1. Impact on price level and real wage rate
   2. Growth rate drops to 2% and stays higher in other countries.
      a. Impact on exports, currency values, short-run employment.

3. MACROECONOMICS

I. Demand for money increases; followed by a rise in real interest rates.
   1. Impact on investment, currency value, and exports
   2. Draw AD/AS model; show change.
   3. Fiscal policy to counteract state of economy
      a. Show output, price level, nominal interest rates, price of bonds
   4. Alternative monetary policy to counter state of economy

II. Open economy with a public sector (G)
   1. 2 methods to calculate GDP and why they equal each other
   2. Nominal GDP rose 4%; what other factors do you need to know before you conclude that the standard of living rose by 4%?

III. Assume an economy at full employment.

1. Net investment increase; show effects on each of the following
    a. AD, capital stock, long-run AS, output
2. How does an increase in net investment affect a country's PPF curve?

4. MACROECONOMICS

I. U.S. economy is in deep recession.
    1. Draw appropriate AD/AS model.
    2. Different effect of increase in spending versus a tax cut
    3. Cut in personal taxes would affect each of the following in the short run:
        a. Consumption, real GDP, imports, and exports.
    4. How would an increase in net investment change AD and AS?

II. A floating currency exchange rate exists between the U.S. and France.
    1. U.S. demand for French goods increases, affecting supply of dollars and dollar value.
    2. Interest rates increase in U.S. but not France
        a. Value of the dollar and quantity of dollars supplied in exchange market

III. Assume an economy with no foreign sector.
    1. Draw a model showing a decrease in the money supply and effect on interest rates.
    2. How did the change affect the three components of AD?
    3. How does the change in AD affect the short-run AD/AS model?
        a. Output and price level

5. MACROECONOMICS

I. Economy has high unemployment.
    1. Keynesian solution of increased government spending; draw AE model
    2. Use AD/AS model to show that the impact of government spending can increase output without inflation (stage 1).
    3. Impact of increased G spending on the money supply and interest rates
    4. Impact of a decrease in corporate taxes

5. Long-run impact of tax cut on corporations
6. Impact on real output
7. Price levels in short-run and long-run

II. Interest rates increase in Europe.
1. Value of U.S. currency relative to European
2. Impact of currency valuations on imports and exports

III. $1,000 of new money deposited into a bank
1. Show a bank's balance sheet
2. Excess reserves
3. Monetary multiplier
4. Why the monetary multiplier may not be maximized

6. MACROECONOMICS

I. Economy has a high rate of unemployment (recession)
1. Fiscal Policy Solution
2. AD/AS demonstrating the resultant output and price level if still below full employment output
3. Fiscal policy impact on short term interest rates
4. FOMC policy for an economy below full employment
5. Draw a short-run money market and AD/AS model to show increase in money supply impact upon interest rates, output, and price level.

II. Determinants of Aggregate Supply (potential long-run real GDP)
1. Labor force
2. Increase in government deficit and a tax cut
3. Decrease in cost of inputs
4. Improvement in education
5. Increase in rate of savings

III. Supply and demand analysis of exports and imports
1. Interest Rates on U.S. Government Bonds increase; Japan's decrease
2. Draw a yen money market model showing impact
3. Domestic price relative to world price; predict for U.S.:
    a. Exports to Japan.
    b. Imports from Japan.

7. MACROECONOMICS

I.   The U.S. is in severe recession with no inflation.
    1.   Draw a labeled AD/AS model for this economy
    2.   Use this graph to show changes due to decrease in government spending
    3.   The effect of the purchase of bonds by the Fed on the economy
        a.   Interest rates
        b.   Output and price levels
        c.   Balance of trade

II.   A country is experiencing severe, unanticipated inflation.
    1.   Effect on those with savings in fixed CD, those with a fixed loan rate
    2.   Fiscal policy action to fight inflation
    3.   FOMC action to fight inflation
    4.   Effect on nominal interest rates if high inflation continues
    5.   Effect on currency values if high inflation is greater than that of other countries

III.   Two countries can produce two products: Country A, 30 cars or 10 tractors, and Country B, 20 cars or 40 tractors
    1.   Which has absolute advantage?
    2.   Which has comparative advantage?
    3.   If specializing, what will each produce?
    4.   What are terms of trade?

APPENDIX B

KEY ECONOMIC FORMULAE

MICROECONOMICS

Allocative Efficiency: Marginal Benefit = Marginal Cost

$P > MC$ = underallocation of resources

$P < MC$ = overallocation of resources

Average Fixed Cost: $(AFC) = \dfrac{\text{Total Fixed Cost (TFC)}}{\text{Quantity of Output (Q)}}$

Average Product: $(AP) = \dfrac{\text{Total Product}}{\text{Units of Input}}$

Average Total Cost: $(ATC) = \dfrac{\text{Total Cost (TC)}}{\text{Quantity of Output (Q)}}$

Average Variable Cost: $(AVC) = \dfrac{\text{Total Variable Cost (TVC)}}{\text{Quantity of Output (Q)}}$

Cross Elasticity of Demand:

$$\dfrac{\text{Percentage of change in Quantity demanded of Good Y}}{\text{Percentage of change in Price of Good X}}$$

I.   If outcome is +, goods are complementary

II. If outcome is −, goods are substitutes

III. If no change in Qd, goods are unrelated

Income Elasticity of Demand:

$$\dfrac{\text{Percentage of change in Quantity demanded of Good}}{\text{Percentage of change in Income}}$$

I.   If outcome is +, good is a normal good

II. If outcome is −, good is an inferior good

Least-Cost Combination of Resource Inputs: $\dfrac{MU_L}{P_L} = \dfrac{MU_C}{P_C}$

Least-Cost Combination/Profit Maximum: $\dfrac{MU_L}{P_L} = \dfrac{MU_C}{P_C} = 1$

Marginal Cost (MC): $\dfrac{\text{Change in Total Cost}}{\text{Change in Quantity Output}}$

Marginal Product (MP): $\dfrac{\text{Change in Total Product}}{\text{Change in Resource Input}}$

Marginal Resource Cost (MRC): $\dfrac{\text{Change in Total Cost}}{\text{Change in Input Quantity}}$

Marginal Revenue (MR): $\dfrac{\text{Change in Total Revenue}}{\text{Change in Quantity Output}}$

Marginal Revenue Product (MRP):

$$\dfrac{\text{Change in Total Revenue}}{\text{Change in Quantity of Resource Input}}$$

Marginal Utility (MU): $\dfrac{\text{Change in Total Utility (Satisfaction)}}{\text{Change in Output Quantity Consumed}}$

Marginal Utility Maximization: $\dfrac{MU_X}{\$P_X} = \dfrac{MU_Y}{\$P_Y} = $ Income Limitation

Price Elasticity: consumer and producer response to price changes

    I.   Of demand:

$$\dfrac{\text{Percentage of Change in Quantity Demanded of Good X}}{\text{Percentage of Change in Price of Good X}}$$

    II.   Of Supply:

$$\dfrac{\text{Percentage of Change in Quantity Supplied of Good X}}{\text{Percentage of Change in Price of Good X}}$$

Productive Efficiency: Price = Marginal Cost = Minimum ATC

Profit: Total Revenue – Total Cost

I. Accounting Profit: Total Revenue – Fixed & Variable Costs (explicit only)

II. Economic Profit: TR – Fixed & Variable Costs (explicit and implicit costs)

III. Normal Profit: TR = TC (explicit and implicit costs)

Profit Maximization/Loss Minimization: MR = MC

Total Product: Total Output of Cumulative Resource Input

Total Revenue Test for Elasticity:

I. If Price goes down and TR goes up, elastic portion of demand curve

II. If Price goes down and TR goes down, inelastic portion of demand curve

MACROECONOMIC

Aggregate Expenditure Multiplier: $\dfrac{1}{(1 \pm MPC)}$ or $\dfrac{1}{MPS}$

Average Propensity to Consume: $\dfrac{Consumption}{Income}$

Average Propensity to Save: $\dfrac{Savings}{Income}$

Balance Budget Multiplier = 1

I. Injection of budget spending is subject to full multiplier.

II. Leakage from government taxation is minus the MPS then subject to multiplier.

III. Gap between spending ($100 million) and an equal tax levy ($100 million) is always equal to the initial spending ($100 million).

IV. Can be inflationary or recessionary.

Consumer price Index (CPI) =

$$\frac{\text{price of a set market basket of g / s for a given year}}{\text{price of same set market basket of g / s from a base year}} \times 100$$

Cyclical Unemployment = Total Unemployment − NRU (Structural + Frictional)

Equilibrium GDP = AE = DI (Real output)

GDP = C + I_g + G + Xn

GDP Gap = Potential GDP − Actual GDP

Marginal Propensity to Consume: $\dfrac{\text{Change in Spending (C)}}{\text{Change in Disposable Income}}$

Marginal Propensity to Save: $\dfrac{1 \pm \text{Change in Spending}}{\text{Change in Disposable Income}}$

Monetary Multiplier = $\dfrac{1}{\text{Required Reserve Ratio}}$

Natural Rate of Unemployment = Structural + Frictional Unemployment

NI = Wages and Salaries + Rents + Proprietor Income + Corporate Profits = GDP

Price Index = $\dfrac{\text{Nominal GDP}}{\text{Real GDP}}$

Real GDP = $\dfrac{\text{Nominal GDP}}{\text{Price Index}}$

Unemployment Rate = $\dfrac{\text{Unemployed}}{\text{Total Labor Force}} \times 100$

GLOSSARY

aggregate demand—shows the total quantity of goods and services consumed at different price and output levels.

aggregate demand/aggregate supply (AD/AS) model—uses aggregate demand and aggregate supply to determine and explain price level, real domestic output, disposable income, and employment.

aggregate expenditure—all spending for final goods and services in an economy: $C + I_g + G + Xn = AE$.

aggregate supply shocks—unexpected, large changes in resource costs that shift an economy's aggregate supply curve.

allocative efficiency—distribution of resources among firms and industries to obtain production quantities of the products most wanted by society (consumers); where marginal cost equals marginal benefit.

appreciation (of the dollar)—an increase in the value of the dollar relative to the currency of another nation, so that a dollar buys more of the foreign currency and thus foreign goods become cheaper; critical to long-run trade equilibrium.

asset—items of monetary value owned by a firm or individual; opposite is liability.

asset demand for money—various amounts of money people want to hold as a store of value; the amount varies inversely with the interest rate; critical to monetary policy.

average fixed cost (AFC)—firm's total fixed cost divided by output.

average product—total output produced per unit of a resource employed (total product divided by the quantity of input).

average total cost (ATC)—firm's total cost divided by output, equal to average fixed cost plus average variable cost (AFC + AVC = ATC).

average variable cost (AVC)—firm's total variable cost divided by output.

balanced-budget multiplier—extent to which an equal change in government spending and taxes changes equilibrium gross domestic product; always has a value of 1, because it is equal to the amount of the equal changes in G and T (T is subject to the MPS of consumers and spending is not).

balance sheet—statement of the assets and liabilities that determines a firm's net (solvency).

barrier to entry—artificial prevention of the entry of firms into an industry.

Board of Governors—seven-member group that supervises and controls the money and banking system; appointed by president to 14-year staggered terms; the Federal Reserve Board.

bond—financial instrument through which a borrower (corporate or government) is contracted to pay the principal at a specified interest rate at a specific date (maturity) in the future; promissory note.

break-even point—output at which a (competitive) firm's total cost and total revenue are equal (TR = TC); an output at which a firm has neither an economic profit nor a loss, at which it earns only a normal profit.

Bretton Woods system—international monetary system developed after the Second World War. Under this system, adjustable pegs were employed, the International Monetary Fund helped stabilize foreign exchange rates, and gold (gold standard set at $35 U.S. per ounce of gold) and the dollar were used as international monetary reserves.

budget deficit—amount by which the spending of the (federal) government exceeds its tax revenues in any year.

budget surplus—amount by which the tax revenues of the (federal) government exceed its spending in any year.

built-in (automatic) stabilizers—programs that react to changes in the business cycle without additional government action, increasing government's budget deficit (or reducing its surplus) during a recession and increasing government's budget surplus (or reducing its deficit) during inflation. Unemployment insurance is one such program.

business cycle—records the increases and decreases in the level of economic activity over periods of time. Consists of expansion (boom), peak, recession (bust or contraction), trough (bottom), and recovery phases. GDP data is generally used to plot this cycle, a lagging indicator.

capital—resources (buildings, machinery, and equipment) used to produce goods and services; also called investment goods.

capital account—section of a nation's international balance-of-payments balance sheet that records foreign purchases of U.S. assets (money in) and U.S. purchases of foreign assets (money out).

capitalism—free market economic system in which property is privately owned and the invisible forces of supply and demand set price and quantity.

cartel—overt agreement among firms (or countries) in an industry to fix the price of a product and establish output quotas.

central bank—government agency whose chief function is the control of the nation's money supply; the Federal Reserve.

change in demand—change in the quantity demanded of a good or service at all prices; a shift of the demand curve to the left (decrease) or right (increase).

change in supply—change in the quantity supplied of a good or service at all prices; a shift of the supply curve to the left (decrease) or right (increase).

circular flow model—flow of resource inputs from households to businesses and of g/s from businesses to households. A flow in the opposite direction of money—businesses to households for inputs and from households to businesses for g/s—occurs simultaneously.

Classical economics—school of macroeconomic generalizations accepted by most economists prior to the depression of the 1930s; a main feature was that the free market economy was self-regulating and would naturally return to full employment levels of output.

collusion—when firms act together (collude) to fix prices, divide a market, or otherwise restrict competition; illegal in the United States.

command system—economic system in which property is publicly owned (means of production) and government uses central economic planning to direct and coordinate economic activities; state-planned economy in which price and quantity are set by government (as in the former USSR).

comparative advantage—determines specialization and exchange rate for trade between nations; based on the nation with the lower relative or comparative cost of production.

competition—Adam Smith's requirement for success of a free market, a market of independent buyers and sellers competing with one another; includes ease of access to and exit from the marketplace.

complementary goods—goods that are used together, so if the price of one falls, the demand for the other decreases as well (and vice versa).

concentration ratio—a simple method of determining a monopoly, which adds the percentage of the total sales of an industry made by the four largest sellers in the industry. If the sum is greater than 50%, the industry is considered a shared monopoly.

conglomerate merger—merger of a firm in one industry with a firm in an unrelated industry.

consumer price index (CPI)—index that measures the prices of a set "basket" of some 300 g/s bought by a "typical" consumer; used by government as a main indicator of the rate of inflation.

consumer surplus—that portion of the demand curve that lies above the equilibrium price level and denotes those consumers that would be willing to buy the g/s at higher price levels.

contractionary fiscal policy—combination of government reduction in spending and a net increase in taxes, for the purpose of decreasing aggregate demand, lowering price levels, and thus controlling inflation.

corporation—legal entity ("like a person") chartered by a state or the federal government; limits liability for business debt to the assets of the firm.

cost-push inflation—when an increase in resource costs shifts the aggregate supply curve inward, resulting in an increase in the price level and unemployment; also termed *stagflation*.

cross elasticity of demand—ratio of the percentage change in quantity demanded of one good to the percentage change in the price of another good. If the coefficient is positive, the two goods are substitute. If the coefficient is negative, they are considered complementary.

crowding-out effect—caused by the federal government's increased borrowing in the money market that results in a rise in interest rates. The rise in interest rates results in a decrease in gross business domestic investment (I_g), which reduces the effectiveness of expansionary fiscal policy.

currency rate of exchange—the price in one domestic currency to purchase a unit of another nation's currency. For example, 1 U.S. dollar buys 1.50 Canadian dollars.

current account—section in a nation's international balance of payments that records its exports and imports of goods and services, its net investment income, and its net transfers.

cyclical deficit—federal budget deficit caused by a recession and the resultant decline in tax revenues.

cyclical unemployment—type of unemployment caused by recession; less than full employment aggregate demand.

deflation—decline in the economy's price level; indicates contraction in business cycle or may signal expansion of total output (aggregate supply moves to the right).

demand—the quantity of a g/s that buyers wish to buy at various prices.

depreciation (of the dollar)—decrease in the value of the dollar relative to another currency, so that the dollar buys a smaller amount of the foreign currency and therefore the price of foreign goods increases; tends to reduce imports and increase exports.

derived demand—orders for a production input that depend on a demand for the product that the input helps to produce.

determinants of demand—factors other than price that alter (shift) the quantities demanded of a good or service.

determinants of supply—factors other than price that alter (shift) the quantities supplied of a good or service.

direct relationship—correlation between two variables that change in the same direction; for example, income and spending.

discount rate—interest rate that the Federal Reserve Banks charge on the loans they make to banks (different from the federal funds rate).

discretionary fiscal policy—deliberate changes in taxes (rates and types) and government spending by Congress.

disposable income—personal income minus personal taxes; income available for consumption expenditures and saving.

dissaving—when spending for consumer g/s exceeds disposable income.

dumping—predatory business practice; sale of products below cost in a foreign country or below the domestic prices.

durable good—consumer good with an expected life (use) of three or more years; decrease in sales indicates recession, as contraction affects these goods before nondurables.

easy money policy—Federal Reserve actions designed to stimulate gross business domestic investment (I_g) and thus aggregate demand; counters recession by increasing the money supply to lower interest rates and expand real GDP.

economic efficiency—use of the minimum necessary inputs to obtain the most societally beneficial quantity of g/s; employs both productive and allocative efficiency.

economic profit—total revenue of a firm minus its economic costs (both explicit and implicit costs); also termed *pure profit* and *above-normal profit*.

economic rent—price paid for the use of land and other natural resources, the supply of which is fixed.

economies of scale—savings in the average total cost of production as the firm expands the size of plant (its output) in the long run.

elastic demand—product or resource demand whose price elasticity is greater than 1. This means that the resulting percentage change in quantity demanded is greater than the percentage change in price.

elastic supply—product or resource supply whose price elasticity is greater than 1. This means that the resulting percentage change in quantity supplied is greater than the percentage change in price.

entitlement programs—government programs, such as social insurance, food stamps, Medicare, and Medicaid, that guarantee benefits to all who fit the programs' criteria.

equilibrium price—price at which the quantity demanded and the quantity supplied are equal (intersect), shelves clear, and price stability occurs.

equilibrium quantity—quantity demanded and supplied at the equilibrium price.

excess capacity—plant resources underused when imperfectly competitive firms produce less output than that associated with achieving minimum average total cost.

exchange rate—trade ratio of one nation's currency for another nation's currency.

expansionary fiscal policy—combination of government increases in spending and a net decrease in taxes, for the purpose of increasing aggregate demand, increasing output and disposable income, and lowering unemployment.

expected rate of return—profit a firm anticipates it will obtain by purchasing capital goods; influences investment demand for money.

explicit cost—payment a firm must make to an outsider to obtain a production input.

factors of production—resources: land, capital, and entrepreneurial ability.

federal funds rate—the interest rate banks and other depository institutions charge one another on overnight loans made out of their excess reserves; targeted by monetary policy.

Federal Open Market Committee (FOMC)—the 12-member group that determines the purchase and sale policies of the Federal Reserve Banks in the market for U.S. government securities; affects federal funds rate.

Federal Reserve Banks—12 banks chartered by the U.S. government to control the money supply and perform other functions such as clearing checks.

Federal Trade Commission (FTC)—commission of five members established by the Federal Trade Commission Act of 1914 to investigate unfair competitive practices of firms, to hold hearings on complaints of such practices, and to issue cease-and-desist orders when firms have been found to have engaged in such practices.

fixed cost—any cost that remains constant when the firm changes its output.

fixed exchange rate—rate of currency exchange that is set, prevented from rising or falling with changes in currency supply and demand; opposite of floating rate.

floating exchange rate—rate of exchange determined by the international demand for and supply of a nation's money; free to increase or decrease.

frictional unemployment—unemployment caused by workers' voluntarily changing jobs or workers' being between jobs.

full employment unemployment rate—natural rate of unemployment when there is no cyclical unemployment. In the United States, equals between 4% and 5%, because some frictional and structural unemployment is unavoidable.

GDP deflator—price index found by dividing nominal GDP by real GDP; used to adjust nominal GDP to real GDP.

General Agreement on Tariffs and Trade (GATT)—international agreement, reached in 1947, in which 23 nations agreed to reduce tariff rates and eliminate import quotas. The Uruguay Round of the GATT talks led to the World Trade Organization.

government transfer payment—money (or g/s) issued to an individual by a government for which the government receives no direct payment from that person.

gross domestic product (GDP)—total market value of all final goods and services produced annually within the boundaries of the United States, whether by U.S. or foreign-supplied resources.

horizontal merger—merger into a single firm of two firms that produce the same product and sell it in the same geographic market.

hyperinflation—a very rapid rise in the price level; an extremely high rate of inflation.

imperfect competition—all market structures except pure competition; includes monopoly, monopolistic competition, and oligopoly.

implicit cost—the monetary income a firm sacrifices when it uses a resource it owns rather than supplying the resource in the market; equal to what the resource could have earned in the best-paying alternative employment; includes a normal profit.

indifference curve—curve showing the different combinations of two products that yield the same satisfaction or utility to a consumer.

inelastic demand—product or resource demand for which the elasticity coefficient for price is less than 1. This means the resulting percentage change in quantity demanded is less than the percentage change in price.

inelastic supply—product or resource supply for which the price elasticity coefficient is less than 1. The percentage change in quantity supplied is less than the percentage change in price.

inferior good—a g/s the consumption of which declines as income rises (and vice versa), with price remaining constant.

inflation—rise in the general level of prices.

inflationary gap—amount by which the aggregate expenditure and schedule must shift downward to decrease the nominal GDP to its full employment noninflationary level.

injection—a way of viewing an increase of a component(s) of aggregate expenditure that may result in an overall increase of aggregate demand; opposite of leakage. Addition of spending such as investment, government purchases, or net exports.

interest—payment for the use of borrowed money.

intermediate goods—products purchased for resale or further processing or manufacturing.

international balance of payments—all the transactions that took place between one nation and those of all other nations during a year.

International Monetary Fund (IMF)—the international association of nations that was formed after the Second World War to make loans of foreign monies to nations with temporary payment deficits and, until the early 1970s, to administer the adjustable pegs. It now mainly makes loans to nations that face possible defaults on private and government loans.

inventories—goods that have been produced but remain unsold.

inverse relationship—the relationship between two variables that change in opposite directions; for example, product price and quantity demanded.

invisible hand—tendency of firms and resource suppliers that seek to further their own self-interests in competitive markets also to promote the interest of society as a whole.

Keynesian economics—macroeconomic generalizations leading to the conclusion that a capitalistic economy is characterized by macroeconomic instability and that fiscal policy and monetary policy can be used to promote full employment, price level stability, and economic growth.

kinked demand curve—demand curve for a noncollusive oligopolist, which is based on the assumption that rivals will follow a price decrease and ignore a price increase.

Laffer Curve—curve relating government tax rates and tax revenues and on which a particular tax rate (between 0 and 100 percent) maximizes tax revenues.

law of demand—the principle that, other things being equal, an increase in the price of a product will reduce the quantity of that product demanded, and conversely for a decrease in price.

law of diminishing marginal utility—the principle that as a consumer increases the consumption of a good or service, the marginal utility obtained from each additional unit of the g/s decreases.

law of diminishing returns—the principle that as successive increments of a variable resource are added to a fixed resource, the marginal product of the variable resource will eventually decrease.

law of increasing opportunity costs—the principle that as the production of a good increases, the opportunity cost of producing an additional unit rises.

law of supply—the principle that, other things being equal, an increase in the price of a product will increase the quantity of that product supplied, and conversely for a price decrease.

leakage—(1) a withdrawal of potential spending from the income-expenditures stream via saving, tax payments, or imports; (2) a withdrawal that reduces the lending potential of the banking system.

least-cost combination of resources—the quantity of each resource a firm must employ to produce a particular output at the lowest total cost; the combination at which the ratio of the marginal product of a resource to its marginal resource cost (to its price if the resource is employed in a competitive market) is the same for the last dollar spent on each of the resources employed.

liability—a debt with a monetary value; an amount owed by a firm or an individual.

liquidity—the ease with which an asset can be converted—quickly—into cash with little or no loss of purchasing power. Money is said to be perfectly liquid, whereas other assets have a lesser degree of liquidity.

long run—time frame necessary for producers to alter resource inputs and increase or decrease output; time frame necessary for adjustments to be made as a result of shifts in aggregate demand and supply.

Lorenz curve—a model that demonstrates the cumulative percentage of population and their cumulative share of income; used to show shifts in income distribution across population over time.

M1, M2, M3—money supply measurements that increasingly broaden the definition of money measured; critical to monetarism and interest rates.

macroeconomics—the portion of economics concerned with the overall performance of the economy; focused on aggregate demand-aggregate supply relationship, and the resultant output, income, employment, and price levels.

marginal benefit—change in total benefit that results from the consumption of one more unit of output.

marginal cost—change in total cost that results from the sale of one more unit of output.

marginal product—change in total output relative to the change in resource input.

marginal propensity to consume—change in consumption spending relative to a change in income.

marginal propensity to save—change in saving relative to a change in income.

marginal revenue—change in total revenue that results from the sale of one more unit of product.

marginal revenue cost (MRC)—change in total cost with the addition of one more unit of resource input for production.

marginal revenue product (MRP)—change in total revenue with the addition of one more unit of resource input for production.

marginal utility—the use a consumer gains from the addition of one more unit of a g/s.

market failure—the inability of the free market to provide public goods; over- or underallocation of g/s that have negative/positive externalities; used to justify government intervention.

Medicaid—entitlement program that finances medical costs for needy individuals.

Medicare—compulsory hospital insurance for the elderly, supplied by federal government through transfer payments of taxed wages.

microeconomics—portion of economics concerned with the individual elements that make up the economy: households, firms, government, and resource input prices.

monetarism—economic belief that the main cause of change in aggregate output and price level is movement in the money supply and the resultant interest rate.

monetary policy—policy basis on which the Federal Reserve influences interest rates through manipulation of the money supply to promote price stability, full employment, and productivity growth.

money—any article (paper note, metal coin) generally accepted as having value in exchange for a g/s.

money supply—defined, measured, and reported as M_1, M_2, M_3.

monopsony—a market structure in which there is only one buyer of a resource input or g/s.

MR = MC principle—law stating that to maximize profit and minimize loss, a firm will produce at the output level where the marginal revenue is equal to the marginal cost.

MRP = MRC formula—equation showing that to maximize profit and minimize loss, a firm will employ a resource input quantity when the marginal revenue product is equal to the marginal resource cost of the resource input.

multiplier—the effect that a change in one of the four components of aggregate expenditure has on GDP.

national (public) debt—money owed by the federal government to owners of government securities, equal to the total amount of money borrowed during all deficit spending.

natural monopoly—an industry in which the economy of scale is so large that one producer is the most efficient least-cost producer; usually regulated by government.

natural rate of unemployment—frictional and structural unemployment, the full employment rate, zero cyclical unemployment.

Neo-classical economics—school of economic thought holding that macroeconomic instability is a short-run event, and that the economy is stable at full employment in the long run because prices and wages automatically adjust for downturns in GDP, causing an eventual return to full employment, noninflationary output.

net export effect—any monetary or fiscal policy action is magnified (+ or −) by the effect that the change in U.S. dollar value (interest rates effect exchange rates) has on import and export prices.

normal good—a g/s the consumption of which increases as income increases (opposite of inferior g/s).

normal profit—where price equals average total cost, and cost includes the implicit cost of entrepreneurial value.

North American Free Trade Agreement (NAFTA)—1993 trade agreement between Canada, the United States, and Mexico, designed to reduce trade barriers over a 15-year period.

oligopoly—a market structure in which a few firms have a large market share and sell differentiated products. In oligopolies, firms tend to have large economies of scale, pricing is mutually dependent, and price wars can occur; there is a kinked-demand curve.

Organization of Petroleum Exporting Countries (OPEC)—a cartel that has control of about 60% of the world's oil and has at times effected severe price change by limiting production quotas.

partnership—an unincorporated firm with shared ownership.

perfectly elastic demand—infinite quantity demanded at a particular price; graphed as a straight horizontal line.

perfectly elastic supply—infinite quantity supplied at a particular price; graphed as a straight horizontal line.

perfectly inelastic demand—quantity demanded does not change in response to a change in price; graphed as a vertical straight line.

perfectly inelastic supply—quantity supplied does not change in response to a change in price; graphed as a horizontal straight line.

Phillips Curve—a model that demonstrates the inverse relationship between unemployment (horizontal) and inflation (vertical axis).

price—the sum of money necessary to purchase a g/s.

Price = MC—in a purely competitive market model, the principle that a firm's demand is perfectly elastic and equal to price, so that a firm will maximize profit when price equals marginal cost if price is equal to or greater than ATC and minimize loss if price is greater than AVC.

price ceiling—a price set below equilibrium by government.

price elasticity of demand—percentage of change in quantity demanded divided by percentage of change in price; measures responsiveness to price changes.

price elasticity of supply—percentage of change in quantity supplied divided by percentage of change in price; measures responsiveness to price changes.

price fixing—illegal collusion between producers to set an above-equilibrium price.

price floor—a price set above equilibrium by government.

producer surplus—that portion of the supply curve that lies below equilibrium price and denotes producers that would bring the g/s to market at even lower prices.

progressive tax—a marginal tax rate system in which the percentage of tax increases as income increases and vice versa (such as U.S. federal income tax brackets).

proportional tax—a flat tax system in which the percentage of tax remains fixed as income changes.

public good—a g/s provided by government for which price does not exclude use and use is indivisible into individual components.

pure competition—market structure in which so many firms produce a very similar g/s that no firm has significant control over market price; a "price taker."

pure monopoly—market structure in which one firm is the sole producer of a distinct g/s and thus has significant control over market price; a "price maker."

quantity demanded—various amounts along a consumer demand curve showing the quantity consumers will buy at various prices.

quantity supplied—various amounts along a producer supply curve showing the quantity producers will sell at various prices.

"real"—an economic measurement (such as GDP or income) that has been adjusted for inflation.

recession—two consecutive business quarters of negative real GDP.

regressive tax—a set tax percentage the average rate of which decreases as the taxpayer's income increases, and vice versa; an example is sales tax.

required reserve ratio—a legally fixed percentage of a bank's reserves (demand deposits) that must be deposited with a Federal Reserve Bank.

Say's Law—a controversial generalization that the production of goods and services creates an equal demand for those g/s. Associated with economic policies under President Reagan.

shortage—difference between the quantity demanded of a g/s and the quantity supplied at a below-equilibrium price ($Q_d > Q_s$).

short run—the length of time during which a producer is unable to alter all the inputs of production.

shut-down point—point at which a firm will cease production because revenue would fall below average variable cost.

sole proprietorship—an unincorporated business owned by an individual.

specialization—concentration of resource(s) in the production of a g/s that results in increased efficiency of production.

spillover benefit—positive externality. Production or consumption results in benefits (such as education) not intended by the market participants.

spillover cost—negative externality. Production or consumption results in costs (such as pollution) not borne by the market participants.

structural unemployment—unemployment resulting from a mismatch of worker skill to demand or location.

subsidy—government financial support for which no direct payment is collected.

substitute—goods or services that are interchangeable. When the price of one increases, the demand for the other increases.

supply-side economics—macroeconomic perspective that emphasizes fiscal policies aimed at altering the state of the economy through I_g (short run) and the aggregate supply (long run).

surplus—difference between the quantity demanded of a g/s and the quantity supplied at an above-equilibrium price ($Q_d < Q_s$).

tariff—a tax on imports/exports.

tax—a required payment of money to government, for which the payer receives no direct g/s.

tight money policy—policy basis on which the Federal Reserve system acts to contract the money supply and increase interest rates, thereby slowing the economy.

trade deficit—amount by which a nation's imports exceed its exports.

trade-off—forgone alternative use of a resource in the production of a g/s.

trade surplus—amount by which a nation's exports exceed its imports.

variable cost—cost of inputs that fluctuates as a firm increases or decreases its output.

World Bank—organization that lends to developing nations to assist them in achieving economic growth.

World Trade Organization (WTO)—group established by the Uruguay Round of the GATT to assist in the promotion of trade and resolution of trade disputes.

ANSWER SHEETS

AP Microeconomics Test

SECTION I

1. Ⓐ Ⓑ Ⓒ Ⓓ Ⓔ		31. Ⓐ Ⓑ Ⓒ Ⓓ Ⓔ	
2. Ⓐ Ⓑ Ⓒ Ⓓ Ⓔ		32. Ⓐ Ⓑ Ⓒ Ⓓ Ⓔ	
3. Ⓐ Ⓑ Ⓒ Ⓓ Ⓔ		33. Ⓐ Ⓑ Ⓒ Ⓓ Ⓔ	
4. Ⓐ Ⓑ Ⓒ Ⓓ Ⓔ		34. Ⓐ Ⓑ Ⓒ Ⓓ Ⓔ	
5. Ⓐ Ⓑ Ⓒ Ⓓ Ⓔ		35. Ⓐ Ⓑ Ⓒ Ⓓ Ⓔ	
6. Ⓐ Ⓑ Ⓒ Ⓓ Ⓔ		36. Ⓐ Ⓑ Ⓒ Ⓓ Ⓔ	
7. Ⓐ Ⓑ Ⓒ Ⓓ Ⓔ		37. Ⓐ Ⓑ Ⓒ Ⓓ Ⓔ	
8. Ⓐ Ⓑ Ⓒ Ⓓ Ⓔ		38. Ⓐ Ⓑ Ⓒ Ⓓ Ⓔ	
9. Ⓐ Ⓑ Ⓒ Ⓓ Ⓔ		39. Ⓐ Ⓑ Ⓒ Ⓓ Ⓔ	
10. Ⓐ Ⓑ Ⓒ Ⓓ Ⓔ		40. Ⓐ Ⓑ Ⓒ Ⓓ Ⓔ	
11. Ⓐ Ⓑ Ⓒ Ⓓ Ⓔ		41. Ⓐ Ⓑ Ⓒ Ⓓ Ⓔ	
12. Ⓐ Ⓑ Ⓒ Ⓓ Ⓔ		42. Ⓐ Ⓑ Ⓒ Ⓓ Ⓔ	
13. Ⓐ Ⓑ Ⓒ Ⓓ Ⓔ		43. Ⓐ Ⓑ Ⓒ Ⓓ Ⓔ	
14. Ⓐ Ⓑ Ⓒ Ⓓ Ⓔ		44. Ⓐ Ⓑ Ⓒ Ⓓ Ⓔ	
15. Ⓐ Ⓑ Ⓒ Ⓓ Ⓔ		45. Ⓐ Ⓑ Ⓒ Ⓓ Ⓔ	
16. Ⓐ Ⓑ Ⓒ Ⓓ Ⓔ		46. Ⓐ Ⓑ Ⓒ Ⓓ Ⓔ	
17. Ⓐ Ⓑ Ⓒ Ⓓ Ⓔ		47. Ⓐ Ⓑ Ⓒ Ⓓ Ⓔ	
18. Ⓐ Ⓑ Ⓒ Ⓓ Ⓔ		48. Ⓐ Ⓑ Ⓒ Ⓓ Ⓔ	
19. Ⓐ Ⓑ Ⓒ Ⓓ Ⓔ		49. Ⓐ Ⓑ Ⓒ Ⓓ Ⓔ	
20. Ⓐ Ⓑ Ⓒ Ⓓ Ⓔ		50. Ⓐ Ⓑ Ⓒ Ⓓ Ⓔ	
21. Ⓐ Ⓑ Ⓒ Ⓓ Ⓔ		51. Ⓐ Ⓑ Ⓒ Ⓓ Ⓔ	
22. Ⓐ Ⓑ Ⓒ Ⓓ Ⓔ		52. Ⓐ Ⓑ Ⓒ Ⓓ Ⓔ	
23. Ⓐ Ⓑ Ⓒ Ⓓ Ⓔ		53. Ⓐ Ⓑ Ⓒ Ⓓ Ⓔ	
24. Ⓐ Ⓑ Ⓒ Ⓓ Ⓔ		54. Ⓐ Ⓑ Ⓒ Ⓓ Ⓔ	
25. Ⓐ Ⓑ Ⓒ Ⓓ Ⓔ		55. Ⓐ Ⓑ Ⓒ Ⓓ Ⓔ	
26. Ⓐ Ⓑ Ⓒ Ⓓ Ⓔ		56. Ⓐ Ⓑ Ⓒ Ⓓ Ⓔ	
27. Ⓐ Ⓑ Ⓒ Ⓓ Ⓔ		57. Ⓐ Ⓑ Ⓒ Ⓓ Ⓔ	
28. Ⓐ Ⓑ Ⓒ Ⓓ Ⓔ		58. Ⓐ Ⓑ Ⓒ Ⓓ Ⓔ	
29. Ⓐ Ⓑ Ⓒ Ⓓ Ⓔ		59. Ⓐ Ⓑ Ⓒ Ⓓ Ⓔ	
30. Ⓐ Ⓑ Ⓒ Ⓓ Ⓔ		60. Ⓐ Ⓑ Ⓒ Ⓓ Ⓔ	

SECTION II

Use this page to write your essay. If additional pages are needed, use your own lined paper.

_____

_____

_____

_____

_____

_____

_____

_____

_____

_____

_____

_____

_____

_____

_____

_____

_____

_____

AP Macroeconomics Test

SECTION I

1. Ⓐ Ⓑ Ⓒ Ⓓ Ⓔ
2. Ⓐ Ⓑ Ⓒ Ⓓ Ⓔ
3. Ⓐ Ⓑ Ⓒ Ⓓ Ⓔ
4. Ⓐ Ⓑ Ⓒ Ⓓ Ⓔ
5. Ⓐ Ⓑ Ⓒ Ⓓ Ⓔ
6. Ⓐ Ⓑ Ⓒ Ⓓ Ⓔ
7. Ⓐ Ⓑ Ⓒ Ⓓ Ⓔ
8. Ⓐ Ⓑ Ⓒ Ⓓ Ⓔ
9. Ⓐ Ⓑ Ⓒ Ⓓ Ⓔ
10. Ⓐ Ⓑ Ⓒ Ⓓ Ⓔ
11. Ⓐ Ⓑ Ⓒ Ⓓ Ⓔ
12. Ⓐ Ⓑ Ⓒ Ⓓ Ⓔ
13. Ⓐ Ⓑ Ⓒ Ⓓ Ⓔ
14. Ⓐ Ⓑ Ⓒ Ⓓ Ⓔ
15. Ⓐ Ⓑ Ⓒ Ⓓ Ⓔ
16. Ⓐ Ⓑ Ⓒ Ⓓ Ⓔ
17. Ⓐ Ⓑ Ⓒ Ⓓ Ⓔ
18. Ⓐ Ⓑ Ⓒ Ⓓ Ⓔ
19. Ⓐ Ⓑ Ⓒ Ⓓ Ⓔ
20. Ⓐ Ⓑ Ⓒ Ⓓ Ⓔ
21. Ⓐ Ⓑ Ⓒ Ⓓ Ⓔ
22. Ⓐ Ⓑ Ⓒ Ⓓ Ⓔ
23. Ⓐ Ⓑ Ⓒ Ⓓ Ⓔ
24. Ⓐ Ⓑ Ⓒ Ⓓ Ⓔ
25. Ⓐ Ⓑ Ⓒ Ⓓ Ⓔ
26. Ⓐ Ⓑ Ⓒ Ⓓ Ⓔ
27. Ⓐ Ⓑ Ⓒ Ⓓ Ⓔ
28. Ⓐ Ⓑ Ⓒ Ⓓ Ⓔ
29. Ⓐ Ⓑ Ⓒ Ⓓ Ⓔ
30. Ⓐ Ⓑ Ⓒ Ⓓ Ⓔ

31. Ⓐ Ⓑ Ⓒ Ⓓ Ⓔ
32. Ⓐ Ⓑ Ⓒ Ⓓ Ⓔ
33. Ⓐ Ⓑ Ⓒ Ⓓ Ⓔ
34. Ⓐ Ⓑ Ⓒ Ⓓ Ⓔ
35. Ⓐ Ⓑ Ⓒ Ⓓ Ⓔ
36. Ⓐ Ⓑ Ⓒ Ⓓ Ⓔ
37. Ⓐ Ⓑ Ⓒ Ⓓ Ⓔ
38. Ⓐ Ⓑ Ⓒ Ⓓ Ⓔ
39. Ⓐ Ⓑ Ⓒ Ⓓ Ⓔ
40. Ⓐ Ⓑ Ⓒ Ⓓ Ⓔ
41. Ⓐ Ⓑ Ⓒ Ⓓ Ⓔ
42. Ⓐ Ⓑ Ⓒ Ⓓ Ⓔ
43. Ⓐ Ⓑ Ⓒ Ⓓ Ⓔ
44. Ⓐ Ⓑ Ⓒ Ⓓ Ⓔ
45. Ⓐ Ⓑ Ⓒ Ⓓ Ⓔ
46. Ⓐ Ⓑ Ⓒ Ⓓ Ⓔ
47. Ⓐ Ⓑ Ⓒ Ⓓ Ⓔ
48. Ⓐ Ⓑ Ⓒ Ⓓ Ⓔ
49. Ⓐ Ⓑ Ⓒ Ⓓ Ⓔ
50. Ⓐ Ⓑ Ⓒ Ⓓ Ⓔ
51. Ⓐ Ⓑ Ⓒ Ⓓ Ⓔ
52. Ⓐ Ⓑ Ⓒ Ⓓ Ⓔ
53. Ⓐ Ⓑ Ⓒ Ⓓ Ⓔ
54. Ⓐ Ⓑ Ⓒ Ⓓ Ⓔ
55. Ⓐ Ⓑ Ⓒ Ⓓ Ⓔ
56. Ⓐ Ⓑ Ⓒ Ⓓ Ⓔ
57. Ⓐ Ⓑ Ⓒ Ⓓ Ⓔ
58. Ⓐ Ⓑ Ⓒ Ⓓ Ⓔ
59. Ⓐ Ⓑ Ⓒ Ⓓ Ⓔ
60. Ⓐ Ⓑ Ⓒ Ⓓ Ⓔ

SECTION II

Use this page to write your essay. If additional pages are needed, use your own lined paper.

_____

_____

_____

_____

_____

_____

_____

_____

_____

_____

_____

_____

_____

_____

_____

_____

_____

_____

AP Microeconomics Test

SECTION I

1.	Ⓐ Ⓑ Ⓒ Ⓓ Ⓔ		31.	Ⓐ Ⓑ Ⓒ Ⓓ Ⓔ
2.	Ⓐ Ⓑ Ⓒ Ⓓ Ⓔ		32.	Ⓐ Ⓑ Ⓒ Ⓓ Ⓔ
3.	Ⓐ Ⓑ Ⓒ Ⓓ Ⓔ		33.	Ⓐ Ⓑ Ⓒ Ⓓ Ⓔ
4.	Ⓐ Ⓑ Ⓒ Ⓓ Ⓔ		34.	Ⓐ Ⓑ Ⓒ Ⓓ Ⓔ
5.	Ⓐ Ⓑ Ⓒ Ⓓ Ⓔ		35.	Ⓐ Ⓑ Ⓒ Ⓓ Ⓔ
6.	Ⓐ Ⓑ Ⓒ Ⓓ Ⓔ		36.	Ⓐ Ⓑ Ⓒ Ⓓ Ⓔ
7.	Ⓐ Ⓑ Ⓒ Ⓓ Ⓔ		37.	Ⓐ Ⓑ Ⓒ Ⓓ Ⓔ
8.	Ⓐ Ⓑ Ⓒ Ⓓ Ⓔ		38.	Ⓐ Ⓑ Ⓒ Ⓓ Ⓔ
9.	Ⓐ Ⓑ Ⓒ Ⓓ Ⓔ		39.	Ⓐ Ⓑ Ⓒ Ⓓ Ⓔ
10.	Ⓐ Ⓑ Ⓒ Ⓓ Ⓔ		40.	Ⓐ Ⓑ Ⓒ Ⓓ Ⓔ
11.	Ⓐ Ⓑ Ⓒ Ⓓ Ⓔ		41.	Ⓐ Ⓑ Ⓒ Ⓓ Ⓔ
12.	Ⓐ Ⓑ Ⓒ Ⓓ Ⓔ		42.	Ⓐ Ⓑ Ⓒ Ⓓ Ⓔ
13.	Ⓐ Ⓑ Ⓒ Ⓓ Ⓔ		43.	Ⓐ Ⓑ Ⓒ Ⓓ Ⓔ
14.	Ⓐ Ⓑ Ⓒ Ⓓ Ⓔ		44.	Ⓐ Ⓑ Ⓒ Ⓓ Ⓔ
15.	Ⓐ Ⓑ Ⓒ Ⓓ Ⓔ		45.	Ⓐ Ⓑ Ⓒ Ⓓ Ⓔ
16.	Ⓐ Ⓑ Ⓒ Ⓓ Ⓔ		46.	Ⓐ Ⓑ Ⓒ Ⓓ Ⓔ
17.	Ⓐ Ⓑ Ⓒ Ⓓ Ⓔ		47.	Ⓐ Ⓑ Ⓒ Ⓓ Ⓔ
18.	Ⓐ Ⓑ Ⓒ Ⓓ Ⓔ		48.	Ⓐ Ⓑ Ⓒ Ⓓ Ⓔ
19.	Ⓐ Ⓑ Ⓒ Ⓓ Ⓔ		49.	Ⓐ Ⓑ Ⓒ Ⓓ Ⓔ
20.	Ⓐ Ⓑ Ⓒ Ⓓ Ⓔ		50.	Ⓐ Ⓑ Ⓒ Ⓓ Ⓔ
21.	Ⓐ Ⓑ Ⓒ Ⓓ Ⓔ		51.	Ⓐ Ⓑ Ⓒ Ⓓ Ⓔ
22.	Ⓐ Ⓑ Ⓒ Ⓓ Ⓔ		52.	Ⓐ Ⓑ Ⓒ Ⓓ Ⓔ
23.	Ⓐ Ⓑ Ⓒ Ⓓ Ⓔ		53.	Ⓐ Ⓑ Ⓒ Ⓓ Ⓔ
24.	Ⓐ Ⓑ Ⓒ Ⓓ Ⓔ		54.	Ⓐ Ⓑ Ⓒ Ⓓ Ⓔ
25.	Ⓐ Ⓑ Ⓒ Ⓓ Ⓔ		55.	Ⓐ Ⓑ Ⓒ Ⓓ Ⓔ
26.	Ⓐ Ⓑ Ⓒ Ⓓ Ⓔ		56.	Ⓐ Ⓑ Ⓒ Ⓓ Ⓔ
27.	Ⓐ Ⓑ Ⓒ Ⓓ Ⓔ		57.	Ⓐ Ⓑ Ⓒ Ⓓ Ⓔ
28.	Ⓐ Ⓑ Ⓒ Ⓓ Ⓔ		58.	Ⓐ Ⓑ Ⓒ Ⓓ Ⓔ
29.	Ⓐ Ⓑ Ⓒ Ⓓ Ⓔ		59.	Ⓐ Ⓑ Ⓒ Ⓓ Ⓔ
30.	Ⓐ Ⓑ Ⓒ Ⓓ Ⓔ		60.	Ⓐ Ⓑ Ⓒ Ⓓ Ⓔ

SECTION II

Use this page to write your essay. If additional pages are needed, use your own lined paper.

_____

_____

_____

_____

_____

_____

_____

_____

_____

_____

_____

_____

_____

_____

_____

_____

_____

_____

AP Macroeconomics Test

SECTION I

1. Ⓐ Ⓑ Ⓒ Ⓓ Ⓔ
2. Ⓐ Ⓑ Ⓒ Ⓓ Ⓔ
3. Ⓐ Ⓑ Ⓒ Ⓓ Ⓔ
4. Ⓐ Ⓑ Ⓒ Ⓓ Ⓔ
5. Ⓐ Ⓑ Ⓒ Ⓓ Ⓔ
6. Ⓐ Ⓑ Ⓒ Ⓓ Ⓔ
7. Ⓐ Ⓑ Ⓒ Ⓓ Ⓔ
8. Ⓐ Ⓑ Ⓒ Ⓓ Ⓔ
9. Ⓐ Ⓑ Ⓒ Ⓓ Ⓔ
10. Ⓐ Ⓑ Ⓒ Ⓓ Ⓔ
11. Ⓐ Ⓑ Ⓒ Ⓓ Ⓔ
12. Ⓐ Ⓑ Ⓒ Ⓓ Ⓔ
13. Ⓐ Ⓑ Ⓒ Ⓓ Ⓔ
14. Ⓐ Ⓑ Ⓒ Ⓓ Ⓔ
15. Ⓐ Ⓑ Ⓒ Ⓓ Ⓔ
16. Ⓐ Ⓑ Ⓒ Ⓓ Ⓔ
17. Ⓐ Ⓑ Ⓒ Ⓓ Ⓔ
18. Ⓐ Ⓑ Ⓒ Ⓓ Ⓔ
19. Ⓐ Ⓑ Ⓒ Ⓓ Ⓔ
20. Ⓐ Ⓑ Ⓒ Ⓓ Ⓔ
21. Ⓐ Ⓑ Ⓒ Ⓓ Ⓔ
22. Ⓐ Ⓑ Ⓒ Ⓓ Ⓔ
23. Ⓐ Ⓑ Ⓒ Ⓓ Ⓔ
24. Ⓐ Ⓑ Ⓒ Ⓓ Ⓔ
25. Ⓐ Ⓑ Ⓒ Ⓓ Ⓔ
26. Ⓐ Ⓑ Ⓒ Ⓓ Ⓔ
27. Ⓐ Ⓑ Ⓒ Ⓓ Ⓔ
28. Ⓐ Ⓑ Ⓒ Ⓓ Ⓔ
29. Ⓐ Ⓑ Ⓒ Ⓓ Ⓔ
30. Ⓐ Ⓑ Ⓒ Ⓓ Ⓔ

31. Ⓐ Ⓑ Ⓒ Ⓓ Ⓔ
32. Ⓐ Ⓑ Ⓒ Ⓓ Ⓔ
33. Ⓐ Ⓑ Ⓒ Ⓓ Ⓔ
34. Ⓐ Ⓑ Ⓒ Ⓓ Ⓔ
35. Ⓐ Ⓑ Ⓒ Ⓓ Ⓔ
36. Ⓐ Ⓑ Ⓒ Ⓓ Ⓔ
37. Ⓐ Ⓑ Ⓒ Ⓓ Ⓔ
38. Ⓐ Ⓑ Ⓒ Ⓓ Ⓔ
39. Ⓐ Ⓑ Ⓒ Ⓓ Ⓔ
40. Ⓐ Ⓑ Ⓒ Ⓓ Ⓔ
41. Ⓐ Ⓑ Ⓒ Ⓓ Ⓔ
42. Ⓐ Ⓑ Ⓒ Ⓓ Ⓔ
43. Ⓐ Ⓑ Ⓒ Ⓓ Ⓔ
44. Ⓐ Ⓑ Ⓒ Ⓓ Ⓔ
45. Ⓐ Ⓑ Ⓒ Ⓓ Ⓔ
46. Ⓐ Ⓑ Ⓒ Ⓓ Ⓔ
47. Ⓐ Ⓑ Ⓒ Ⓓ Ⓔ
48. Ⓐ Ⓑ Ⓒ Ⓓ Ⓔ
49. Ⓐ Ⓑ Ⓒ Ⓓ Ⓔ
50. Ⓐ Ⓑ Ⓒ Ⓓ Ⓔ
51. Ⓐ Ⓑ Ⓒ Ⓓ Ⓔ
52. Ⓐ Ⓑ Ⓒ Ⓓ Ⓔ
53. Ⓐ Ⓑ Ⓒ Ⓓ Ⓔ
54. Ⓐ Ⓑ Ⓒ Ⓓ Ⓔ
55. Ⓐ Ⓑ Ⓒ Ⓓ Ⓔ
56. Ⓐ Ⓑ Ⓒ Ⓓ Ⓔ
57. Ⓐ Ⓑ Ⓒ Ⓓ Ⓔ
58. Ⓐ Ⓑ Ⓒ Ⓓ Ⓔ
59. Ⓐ Ⓑ Ⓒ Ⓓ Ⓔ
60. Ⓐ Ⓑ Ⓒ Ⓓ Ⓔ

SECTION II

Use this page to write your essay. If additional pages are needed, use your own lined paper.

INDEX

ABOUT THE AUTHOR

Richard Sattora is an AP Economics teacher at Excelsior Award-winning Pittsford Mendon High School, Pittsford, N.Y., where he has taught for 30 years. The caliber of his work has brought Mr. Sattora recognition from *Who's Who Among America's Teachers* and the Federal Reserve Bank of Dallas, where he was designated a "Blue Ribbon Teacher of Economics." He has traveled extensively throughout Europe and led student tours to Eastern Europe and the Soviet Union before the fall of communism. Teaching economics has been Mr. Sattora's focus since 1986. A graduate of Canisius College, he holds an M.S. degree from Nazareth College.

Mr. Sattora's varied background in economics gives him a balanced perspective on the subject. He has worked for Eastman Kodak Co., and been involved in many entrepreneurial activities in the real estate, restaurant, and landscaping fields. He is a member of the Rochester Area Council of Social Studies and the Association of Private Enterprise Educators. His Federal Reserve Challenge Teams have won the right to represent the Federal Reserve Bank of New York's Buffalo Branch numerous times in this prestigious national economics competition.

FROM THE AUTHOR

I would like to thank my wife, Jeanette, and sons Jeffrey and Christopher, whose patience and support allowed this work to be completed. Also, the staff of the Federal Reserve Bank of Dallas, especially Wayne Hast, whose generosity and support for high school economics teachers allowed me to attend my first APEE conference, beginning this journey. Other members of the Federal Reserve Bank of Dallas, including President Bob McTeer, Chief Economist C. Michael Cox, and economist Bob Formiani, continue to educate and inspire me with their presentations and writings. Finally, I would like to thank the staff of the Federal Reserve Branch Bank of Buffalo—Economist Richard Dietz, Reggie Melson, and Connie Poniatowski—for their support of my Federal Reserve Challenge Team.

Richard Sattora
Pittsford Mendon High School
Pittsford, New York

THE BEST TEST PREPARATION FOR THE

AP*

ADVANCED
PLACEMENT
EXAMINATION

UNITED STATES HISTORY

6 Full-Length Practice Exams

Based on official exams released by the College Board

Detailed explanations to every exam question

Far more comprehensive than any other test preparation book

Includes a **COMPREHENSIVE REVIEW COURSE** of the topics covered on the exam. This book can be used for self-study or by any class preparing for the exam.

REA *Research & Education Association*

* AP is a registered trademark of the
College Entrance Examination Board,
which does not endorse this book.

Available at your local bookstore or order directly from us by sending in coupon below.

THE BEST TEST PREPARATION FOR THE

AP

**ADVANCED
PLACEMENT
EXAMINATION**

EUROPEAN HISTORY

6 Full-Length Practice Exams

Based on official exams released by the College Board

Detailed explanations to every exam question

Far more comprehensive than any other test preparation book

Includes a **COMPREHENSIVE REVIEW COURSE** of the topics covered on the exam. This book can be used for self-study or by any class preparing for the exam.

REA *Research & Education Association*

AP is a registered trademark of the
College Entrance Examination Board,
which does not endorse this book.

Available at your local bookstore or order directly from us by sending in coupon below.